MindBuilders'
Play Ma

MindBuilders' Play Manual

Practical Ideas for healthy Development, Play and Behaviour at Home

Sibylle Janert

Confidentiality
In order to ensure overall privacy and anonymity, no names
have been mentioned and identities have been disguised
where appropriate.

Published in March 2012 by MindBuilders, A Not-for-profit
Company Limited by Guarantee, Reg. Nr. 5916235
Correspondence address: www.mindbuilders-consulting.org

ISBN 978 0 9557866 4 8

Layout and Design: trockenbrot (Claudia Schenk)

Printed by: Henry Ling Limited, UK

Contents

4   Playing and Autism

Introduction

About this Book

This book is a collection of very practical suggestions for a healthy home environment with ideas for activities that encourage interactive and social play in families, between parents and their children. Its focus is on activities for younger children, or children who function developmentally like a younger child, as do many children with autism, because we all now know that: 'the earlier the better' because 'the brain does not wait'.

This book is full of practical ideas for interactive play in families and a healthy home environment

Who is this book for?

This is not another book on parenting. There are already so many good parenting guides around. Perhaps too many. However, most of them are written for readers with good educational background, good English, literacy, reading and other skills like those who will go into a bookshop to look for a book on parenting or child development. But not everybody has these skills, - for all sorts of complex reasons (e.g. dyslexia, migration, asylum-seekers, immigration, especially from non-urban out-door child-raising backgrounds, not confident in speaking/reading English, etc.). It is these families above all, who this book is for. The images add a level of meaning that words alone cannot provide, and I hope these reflect the wide range of families and cultures I have encountered and learnt from, and who were happy to share their pictures.

This book is for and from families who like pictures

Why I created this picture manual/ book

This book is a response to the questions and problems I have encountered again and again over many years in my early autism intervention work with families as funded by London Borough of Tower Hamlets. It tries to give practical answers to what parents have told or shown me they need to know in order to help their children to grow up well, to catch up with developmental delay or to deal with certain behaviour problems. In families, where there is a lack of structure in terms of space and time and daily routines, or with a child with autistic behaviours, this is even more difficult. However, as I have experienced repeatedly, with the appropriate kind of attention, interest, encouragement, environmental and family support (as described in the family chapter), many children with an autism diagnosis can make amazing progress. Many of these families live in poor and overcrowded urban housing conditions, often with many additional challenges. But the issues raised in this book relate just as much to families living in better conditions, who I have in fact found to struggle with

This book was inspired by families living in urban housing conditions

more of less the same (modern?) issues despite having more 'stuff' or money.

By helping parents to know how to help their child at home, this book aims to empower parents and to reduce reliance on sometimes similarly impoverished and cash-strapped external services. This is how the Play Manual was really born: to provide families with a wide range of activities and ideas, where they can get ideas and inspiration.

Empowering parents to use their own resources reduces reliance on cash-strapped external services

'But I don't know how to play with him!': How to use this book

The idea of this book is to give parents and children ideas for interactive play and communication. It is not the kind of book that is meant to be read from beginning to end, or page by page. It is meant for dipping in and finding something that gives the reader some ideas and stimulates their thinking. So often I have heard parents of an autistic child say 'But he won't play with me' or 'I just don't know what to do'. It is at such times, that I hope that the pictures, descriptions and lists of ideas will help and inspire you!

Open the book somewhere and let yourself be surprised and inspired!

Sibylle Janert and MindBuilders' Approach How to build a healthy mind?

In this book I have tried to describe some of the main influences on my way of working. My interest has always been how the mind develops and what goes on in a person's internal world, whether adult, child, baby, mentally healthy or confused, with developmental challenges or diagnosed as autistic. How does the mind develop and build itself? How can parents help their children to build healthy internal mental structures and to manage well what goes on inside their mind, and inside the family? This is what MindBuilders aims to focus on.

How does the mind develop and build itself?

Babies know more than you may think – Families are complex – Parenting is difficult

My training and teaching of emotionally-informed Infant-in-the-Family Observation (Tavistock Clinic, Terapia) showed me how incredibly communicative, perceptive and competent already tiny babies are, - and how difficult it is to be a parent. I realised how everyone in a family is affected by what happens to any individual in the family, i.e. if there is stress on the family system by a child's difficult behaviours or a parent's depression, then each member will experience and have to adjust to the stress. I have been very much influenced by W.R. Bion's 'Theory of Thinking' and by those who developed his ideas on the unconscious processes that go on inside the human mind as well as in groups and families, in particular Frances Tustin, Anne Alvarez, Franco Scabbiolo and many others.

A cheap cat-litter tray is ideal for playing with water or sand at home

Movement is a child's first language

Babies and children learn from doing and moving. By exploring their environment, children learn about themselves and their bodies in relation to the world around them. But in our modern world, people spend more and more time immobile, sitting in the car, on the settee, in front of computer, TV or mobile. Children and adults move less and less, with the very detrimental effects, especially for children's physical, mental and language development. For the formative brain development in babies the immobile passivity induced by electronic media and press-the-button 'toys' is an unmitigated disaster.

DIR: A universal Approach
Developmental – Individualized – Relationship-based

When I then encountered the DIR-Floortime model, it was amazing. Its Functional Emotional Developmental Levels (FEDL) provide such a helpful framework for identifying, understanding and addressing a child's developmental difficulties, using a universal and totally inclusive model of mental-emotional development. Home Office funding from the Community Development Foundation allowed me to train with Dr. Rick Solomon in Michigan/USA in 2007 to become the first qualified PLAY-Home Consultant in the UK to coach parents to play and communicate more effectively with their autistic child at home. In fact, this model of developmentally informed therapeutic home consultations focusing on play is so effective and helpful to parents overall that it should be made available to all families struggling with developmental or behavioural issues with their child.

Acknowledgements

I wish to thank all the families, children and parents for their generosity, letting me learn with them and share their experiences, photos, videos and stories. This book could not have been written without the invaluable support, teaching and supervision of many of my colleagues. I am particularly grateful to Franco Scabbiolo, for his unwavering interest, support, 'thinking help' and thought-provoking contributions that have greatly influenced both my mind and my work. I am indebted to Dr. Rick Solomon and Carol Mannion for their generous support and input over the past years. I am most grateful to Khalida Khan, Integrated Service Manager of the Disabled Children's Team of the London Borough of Tower Hamlets, for her understanding, support and commitment to my and MindBuilders' work with local families, without which this book would not have happened and to Claudia Schenk's amazing 'yes we can' approach. I am indebted to innumerable books and papers for providing information and knowledge. And thank you to Awards for All for funding this project.

Balance bikes promote brain development by helping the child learn about their body

The DIR-Floortime model gives us a clear sense of direction for development

Learning new activities and sharing experiences at a MindBuilders' workshop

1 Playing at MindBuilders

Building the internal world of our mind

Building and managing our mind is the most important, but also the most difficult task for human beings. It is a life-long effort that starts before we are born and continues to the end of our lives. The human mind is full of thoughts and feelings that are the building materials of the internal world of our personality, and connected with our experiences and relationships with our external and inner worlds. Our experiences with the outside world affect our internal world (and vice versa), i.e. what happens at home, whether there are supportive relationships with people, who provide love, guidance as well as structure and predictable routines in an environment that is safe and interesting to explore, makes all the difference to the development of the mind and brain of a baby and growing child. External space always also has aspects of a symbolic communication: being in a warm, bright and cozy space makes us feel different than being in a chaotic, cold or neglected space. The same is true for our relationship with time, especially for children whose sense of time is still developing. Knowing who is expected to do what, when and in what order gives a comforting sense of reassurance and increases confidence. Too much of a 'laissez-faire approach' in families or what I call 'The Whatever Attitude' to mental development, i.e. not enough guidance and thoughtful support from parents to their children's developmental needs, invariably results in chaos, confusion, degradation, depression and despair, because the human mind is also so fragile and in need of careful attention and care.

In essence, human mental life is made up of relationships with space and time, in the outside world and in our internal emotional world. But sometimes we feel that we can't get in. Often we feel stuck or trapped and can't get out. This is often the predominant feeling when in the presence of a child with aggressive, repetitive or puzzling autistic behaviours: we feel trapped, and the child too seems to be stuck and unable to move on. How can we get out? And how to get the child out of that constricting state of mind? We need strategies to organise our internal mental space and to manage our internal emotional relationships within it. These strategies require 'thinking'. The 'motor' that starts the required thinking (higher brain functions) are our thoughts and emotions (lower brain functions), and the mind has to develop inside itself a container for dealing with these emotions, feelings, thoughts and internal relationships. How space and time are organised is in

Building our minds is a creative process that requires careful attention

Our mind has to develop an internal container for dealing with our thoughts and feelings

fact like a grammar, and therefore crucial for healthy mental, social and language development.

When mental development gets stuck:
Developmental delay, autism and other states of mind

Parents with a child with developmental delay or special needs often feel isolated, alone and unsupported in their sense of helplessness. The child seems developmentally stuck. Parents and other adults tend to feel trapped by the challenging or puzzling behaviours and feelings that surround them. When they seek help, they often complain about public services being slow to listen and respond, lack of personalised attention, time and resources, - often due to the deficit-oriented and crisis-driven nature of our current systems with their focus on pathologising and diagnosing. As a result, professionals tend to focus more on the child's 'deficit' or diagnostic label than on understanding the complexities of the whole personality and the contextual nature of mental development and growing up. But with suitable support that is well enough informed and comes early enough, babies and children with developmental delay can always make progress, especially when parents are actively involved, - and nobody knows the limits of anyone's potential.

Children with an autism diagnosis are first of all children like any other child

Despite the appearance of the certainty of diagnosis, there appears to be wide-spread confusion about the differences or overlaps of developmental delay, autism, challenging behaviours, attachment problems, early sensory deprivation, infantile post-traumatic stress disorder, parenting difficulties, temperament and personality differences, etc. While the diagnosis of autism is increasing, there are often differing opinions, and we all know children with an autism diagnosis that is contested by others. However, there is of course always a problem that parents seeking help with and that needs addressing in very real and practical ways, - at home and by parents.

   In this book, autism is seen as a continuum within a child's developmental path, not just as a 'defect' in the child's biology. Although there is one word, there is actually no overall agreement on what 'autism' is exactly. I therefore use the words 'autism' - 'autistic' - 'with an autism diagnosis' pretty much interchangeably, because looking at the child as a child first of all and in the context of his family matters more than the label given to his differences or 'problems'. In my experience, autism does not have to be a life-long condition (although it often is). But it certainly does not need to be the life-sentence it is usually portrayed as. Whatever autism is, the child with autism has a mind that can change, grow and

TV-zombies: Stuck in a self-absorbed state of mind without interaction or movement

Caught on the see-saw between the diagnosis of autism and addressing the child's actual issues

develop with the same infinite potential of any other human being, given the right support and conditions. The crucial question is that of building, maintaining and using the mind to the best of each child's abilities. If we can help the child to be able to think and understand the world around him, to make sense of his internal and external world, and to relate to other people, ... then he can go anywhere in the world!

A child's family is the best place for supporting a child's development

The mind building function of the family for EVERY child

Babies and children need a family in order to grow up well. All children need space to play, things to explore, realistic expectations as well as attention, encouragement and genuine interest from parents at home for their child's individual personality. This is equally true for families with a child with an autism diagnosis or other developmental delay or disability, who in fact needs this just as much, or even more so, than their siblings or any other child. In families, where parents receive help to address their child's need for structure at home, clear boundaries and daily routines, to keep control of TV and other electronic devices (i.e. off for most of the day!) and focus instead on interactive and non-materialistic play and movement activities, behaviour problems get under control and family life becomes more relaxed and happy.

Play matters:
Play is to early childhood what petrol is to a car.

Play is for a child what work is for the adult, or 'Play is to early childhood what petrol is to a car': it is play that drives children's development. Children's need to play is now even supported by the United Nations Convention of the Rights of the Child. But not everyone understands about the importance of play for all areas of a child's development, and modern children increasingly spend their time with electronic devices instead of actively playing, exploring and interacting with the world and people around them. As I try to illustrate in this book, play is also the best way to help children with developmental delay or additional needs, including autism, because it promotes brain and mental growth through emotional engagement and relationships with other people. Lack of play is dangerous for all children and our whole society, because the child misses out on crucial and mind-building experiences. It is like 'pulling the humanising rug from under humanity's feet' says Bob Hughes, an expert on play, resulting in play deprivation and the human child version of battery chickens: 'battery children'.

Interactive play promotes brain development and mental growth

2 Playing with Babies

Play is a Basic Need, even for tiny Babies

Babies can and want to play from the moment they are born, – or even before.

Long before the baby has physical control over his body, long before he can hold a toy in his hand, and already a few days after birth, babies reach out with their eyes to follow and explore what is around them in an interested and playful way.

But in order to play successfully, a tiny baby needs a play-partner to respond to their invitations to play.

Babies need an adult to attune closely to their developmental level, temperament and current mood.

*Perhaps the most important baby-game is when the adult pays close attention to what the baby is paying attention to, experiencing, watching or looking at, and says this in words: 'I (baby) look – **you** (adult) say'*

Babies
→ can play from birth onwards
→ are born with a stunning capacity for interaction, curiosity and playfulness
→ want to socialise and 'talk' with other people from birth, and even before
→ talk through their behaviours, eye-pointing and by using non-verbal body-language
→ need someone to pay good attention to their gestures, movements and feelings and listen to what they are trying to tell you

It is in the first 3-4 months that babies learn how to initiate, maintain, end or avoid contact with another person, which means how to relate to, communicate and play with other people, and later on how to relate to and play with toys.

True symbolic play, imaginatively or with toys, as well as school-learning only becomes possible once the infant has had enough of those experiences of being with another person, of being taken seriously as well as enjoying playful interactions with other people.

... from the moment they are born ...

Newborn responding with interest in eyes and face to the adult's delighted face and tone of voice

Even a tiny baby can play a version of 'Catch!' and 'Hide and seek' with their eyes or by making sounds and trading them back and forth with the adult

Games to Play with your Baby

'People-Games' are the earliest attempts at play and playfulness, starting from birth or before.

→ People-games are essential for all later development of symbolic play, language and relationships.
→ Being purely social games, they are the best and the cheapest games you can play with your baby, as they need no equipment and cost no money.
→ All that is needed is for the other person to pay good attention, to listen and to observe with interest.
→ Tune in to what the baby is feeling, interested in and trying to tell you through his movements, sounds, gestures, smiles and other behaviours.

Dialogue Games

'Dialogue games are the first games parents and infants play together.' (Newson 1979)

→ The everyday little 'conversations' between mother and baby are almost purely social in nature and in which the eyes of both players are the most important.
→ Many of these interactions take place while the adult is feeding, changing, bathing or comforting the baby.
→ At other times babies love to play little interaction games for no other reason than to be with and to enjoy each other's company.
→ Playing like this allows the baby to explore action patterns, rhythm, sequencing and to learn about turn-taking, all essential building-blocks for language-development.
→ Later this will also include nursery rhymes like 'Pat-a-cake' and 'Round and round the garden', playfully repeated again and again.

Mirroring Games

→ Mirror and echo what your baby does in order to create a simple form of dialogue.
→ You can copy his sounds softly and add some new sounds, trading sounds back and forth as if it were a ball.
→ You can copy the rhythm, with which he bangs his foot or hand. You can also bang it with your hand, on the cot or on his body. Or you can SAY his foot-rhythm with your sounds, e.g. 'Bang bang bang, says baby. – Bang bang bang, says mummy.'

Face-to-Face 'Looming Games'

What captivates a baby most in a person is their face, especially their eyes. Faces are alive, moving and changing all the time, showing us what goes on inside someone, their

Babies respond with delight to a tuned-in person making funny noises and faces

Talk WITH and talk FOR your Baby:
→ *Say what your baby would say, if he could talk*
→ *Let him hear his intentions and ideas spoken out loud*
→ *Match what he has in mind using your tone of voice and describing words*

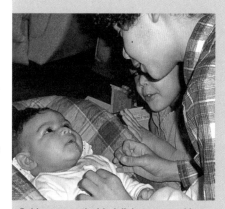

Babies respond with delight to a tuned-in person talking to them

Mirroring each other's smiles, sounds and movements makes baby feel understood

feelings and intentions. From the earliest age your baby will search out his or her mother's (or father's) eyes and study her face for long periods of time, initially mainly while feeding, but by about 6 weeks increasingly at other times to initiate social play interactions.

→ These games may be started either by the baby or his mother.
→ One of the players will look at the other to check out their readiness to play and their emotional state.
→ If either of the 2 players breaks gaze, the game is over.
→ If the game is going to take place, the other will notice this look, experience it as an invitation and respond by looking back.
→ Both will then make a 'greeting-face': eye-brows raised, eyes widened, mouth opened and head moving back, as in a mock-surprise expression.
→ They will also take up a full-face position and concentrate all their attention on the other person and their face.
→ The baby can regulate such face-to-face interactions effectively in many ways: he can expand them with smiles, refuse by averting or closing his eyes, terminate by turning his head away, etc.
→ By playing like this, the baby learns about his own capacities to influence what goes on, to start and terminate what the adult does, to make her face come and go by looking, turning his head or closing his eyes.

By the age of 4.5 months it might go something like this: 'Joey is sitting on his mother's lap, facing her. She looks at him intently but with no expression on her face, as if she were preoccupied and absorbed in thought elsewhere. At first, he glances at the different parts of her face but finally looks into her eyes. He and she remain locked in a silent mutual gaze for a long moment. She finally breaks it by easing into a slight smile. Joey quickly leans forward and returns her smile. They smile together; or rather they trade smiles back and forth several times.

Then Joey's mother moves into a game-like sequence. She opens her face into an expression of exaggerated surprise, leans all the way forward, and touches her nose to his, smiling and making bubbling sounds all the while. Joey explodes with delight but closes his eyes when their noses touch. She then reels back, pauses to increase the suspense, and sweeps forward again to touch noses. Her face and voice are even more full of delight and 'pretend' menace. This time Joey is both more tense and excited. His smile freezes. His expression moves back and forth between pleasure and fear.

Joey's mother seems not to have noticed the change in him. After another suspenseful pause, she makes a third

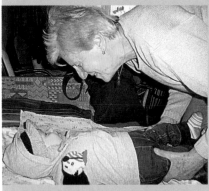
Everyone plays 'looming games' with baby who are fascinated watching a playful face come close and retreat

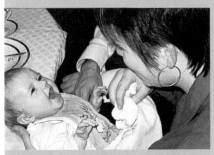
Babies love 'face-to-face' games

Baby inviting the adult into a conversation-game with her eyes and early speech sounds

nose-to-nose approach at an even higher level of hilarity, and lets out a rousing 'oooOH !' Joey's face tightens. He closes his eyes and turns his head to the side. His mother realises that she has gone too far, and stops her end of the interaction, too. At least for a moment, she does nothing. Then she whispers to him and breaks into a warm smile. He becomes re-engaged.' (Stern 1991)

Peekaboo Games

All children love peekaboo games and babies are no exception.

There is so much to explore for babies in their parents' faces

→ Peekaboo games can be played almost everywhere, with the adult's or baby's hands, with a towel at bath-time, while changing a nappy or reading a story.
→ The topic of peekaboo games is disappearance and rediscovery, helping the baby to trust that mother still exists even when she is out of sight, leading to what is called 'object-permanence'.

Both players try to sustain interest and delight, and not to transgress each other's tolerance for frustration. They both concentrate on an 'optimal range'- band of interaction, and the excitement and pleasure over the stimulation keeps their attention focused.

However, transgressions happen all the time, as when mum surprises the baby by appearing sooner than expected, or by stretching out the suspense and keeping the baby on tenterhooks until she … finally … and suddenly … re-appears!

Peekaboo games are about 'there' and 'gone'

BABIES ARE FASCINATED BY MOUTHS:
• Mouths can open and shut.
• Inside the mouth there is a wiggly soft tongue that can go in and out, and wet saliva.
• Adult's mouths also have white hard teeth.
• Mouths are red at the front and dark at the back.
• Mouths are for eating and tasting food and drink.
• Babies love to put their fingers or other things inside the mouth.
• One can use the mouth for making all sorts of different sounds
• Already toothless mouths can bite and hold something between the gums.

Mouth and Face Games

Babies are fascinated by faces, eyes and mouths, because faces are always moving and changing. They show us what the person is thinking and feeling. They can make sounds and surprising noises. They can talk, conveying their thoughts in language that has a music all of its own, depending on culture and personality of the speaker. Already babies can recognise a person when hearing their voice. Eyes can shine with delight or go dark with sad feelings. Mouths can do so many things. There is so much to learn and explore, if you allow your baby to explore your face.

Feeding a baby is already a conversation between mother and baby, – or: it should be!

→ Pay attention to your tone of VOICE: you can make it go UP and DOWN, go SLOW and FAST, or do it suddenly
→ Use your own body-language and tone of voice like a cat to 'CREEP up' on him gently and suddenly 'POUNCE' and surprise him, in a fun way, when he wasn't expecting it.
→ Make funny noises with your mouth or tongue
→ Do it behind him, so he has to turn around.
→ Wiggle your tongue: up – down, side to side, in – out
→ Blow raspberries, plop your lips, ...
→ Blow out your cheeks ... blow out ONE cheek only and let him pop it ... then the other
→ Bare your teeth ... or clatter your teeth 3x, then stop and wait for him to copy ...
→ Pretend to want to bite her fingers ... or nose ... or ear ... or toes ... making gentle growling noises (but be very sensitive not to scare him and stop if he looks frightened!)

Feeding with eye contact

Feeding Games

Making sure to use feeding times as times to communicate and talk with your baby helps to prevent later eating-problems/ eating-disorders. Feeding and eating are, and need to be, communicative social activities. It is not just a matter of putting food into the child like petrol into a car. The child needs to enjoy engaging and interacting with the person giving the food and to be allowed to explore different foods with his hands and all his senses.

Enjoying a feeding conversation together

→ Remember that breast feeding or giving a bottle is also a feeding-conversation with your baby.
→ Respond when he touches you with his hands or when he looks at your eyes.
→ Jiggle him a little, when he stops drinking, then stop when he starts sucking again. It's a feeding game.
→ Seek eye-contact when you are feeding him, and feed his mind with your smiles and adoration in your face.
→ Talk about the food or about what or how the baby is eating. These are all early language experiences.

NEVER prop up your baby's bottle or encourage him to drink it all alone by himself! Doing this is harmful for a baby's mental-emotional development, because feeding and eating are SOCIAL activities. You are NOT putting petrol into a car! This is not the time to encourage independence, which starts with finger-food and using a spoon. Wait for him to tell you, when he is ready to feed himself.

Children also don't need to sit in their buggies constantly attached to a bottle: it stops them from looking around or exploring other things they can do to comfort themselves, i.e. from learning that they can wait a few minutes until you have time to sit together and give them their food as a nice social and shared experience.

Switch off the TV when feeding your baby/child and during mealtimes, so he can look at your face instead at the constantly flickering movement on the screen and listen to your voice when you talk to him rather than to the noises from the TV. After all his mum's/dad's face and voice are the most beautiful thing in the world to a baby. Feeding a young child without awareness to what he is eating in front of a TV-screen or any other electronic device can often lead to feeding and eating problems.

Sucking: Some babies have a greater need for sucking than others, which helps them with self-regulation and to calm themselves down. Some use their thumb or fingers, others a dummy. But all need to learn to let go of the dummy in order for their mouth to be free and ready for other food and for talking. It is best to limit dummies for bedtime or when very upset.

Baby-bottles and dummies for too long
→ If used too much or all the time, bottles and dummies can inhibit speech development.
→ Mouth and tongue muscles need to be strengthened and the tongue needs free mobility in the mouth in order to play and explore making all the different sounds that are necessary for speaking.
→ Constant daytime sucking (e.g. bottles, dummies, sweets, drinks) can prevent a child from attending to everyday life as they can go into reveries or cut off from engaging with others.
→ Over reliance on milk from baby-bottles above the age of 2 years can result in nutrient deficiencies because the child lacks the appetite and interest to explore eating other foods.

By having his bottle all alone, this boy is losing out on eating as a shared and social activity

Dummies can delay a baby's speech development, when used too much

Bottles are for babies meals not constant daytime sucking

Rhymes and Singing

Rhymes and songs are the natural continuation of all of the games above and ideal in fostering social relationships and language-development. They have a clear beginning, middle and end, which helps with the early learning of sequence and predictability and building a structure in your baby's mind. If you wait, your baby will 'tell you' to do it again or even fill in the next word or movement.

Rhymes and songs thrive on rhythm and repetition, which helps with remembering and wanting to say it again. Repetition is very important for all learning and babies love you to do it again ... and again ... and again. Babies and small children have a great need for repetition, and we usually need to sing a song or play a game over and over, and for much longer than we may think until the baby becomes bored, because he has now become familiar with it, and ready to move on.

First the baby will try to communicate to you that he wants you to do it again. Then he will want to 'do it together', with you leaving spaces for him to say the bits that he can say, until a little later, when he will want to say the rhyme or sing the song by himself.

MindBuilders' Rhyme cards will also give you ideas for songs and pictures to talk about. You can read more about them in the section on 'Playing and autism', but they are suitable for all small children.

Movement Games

Movement is really a child's first language. Babies need to explore the world around them, first their own body, then the world of objects through adults providing everyday objects that are interesting for a baby to touch, hold, suck and investigate with all his senses. Already this requires movement. But once the child has become more mobile, he must be allowed to move about so he can encounter more of the world around him. This is essential for learning and healthy brain development, including language and play. Children, who have not gone through the natural experience of all these developmental movement stages, need to catch up with what they have missed (see also our section: 'Every child can learn').

The brain feeds on experience of joyful interaction with others

Babies need to explore their own body first

Crawling requires complex coordination of arms, legs, eyes and mind, crucial for healthy brain development, but also for learning to read and write

Physical development:

→ Mouthing and exploring with his mouth
→ Bringing hands together
→ Raising head and chest when lying on tummy
→ Grasping, shaking, banging objects
→ Rolling over (by themselves)
→ Sitting (without support)
→ Transferring an object from one hand to the other
→ Reaching and stretching to reach and grasp something
→ Crawling
→ Picking up and dropping objects
→ Posting objects
→ Pulling himself up to stand and holding on
→ Throwing objects
→ Pointing to show and share with you what he sees (starts around 1 year old)
→ Walking

Crawling allows the child to explore more of the world

The best Play and Activity Centre ever: Treasure Baskets

Part of the new Curriculum for Babies aged 5-12 Months

What is a Treasure Basket?

Treasure Baskets are based on ideas by Eleanor Goldschmied (see book (2004): 'People under 3') and consist of a strong basket (about 30cm in diameter) filled with about 100 everyday and natural things (no plastic or toys) of different size, material, shape, feel, weight, smell, taste and sound. It needs to be about the height of a mug so the baby can safely lean on it for support.

A treasure basket full of everyday and natural objects allows babies to explore ...

TREASURE BASKETS

- **allow baby to explore without adult's interference**
- **support all areas of a baby's physical, emotional and social development including attachment, speech and language, sense of self, confidence, play, thinking and learning**
- **are high-quality low-cost stimulation for babies**
- **provide a chance for the adult to observe and understand each baby's unique personality, interests, skills**

Babies communicating and observing each other while exploring a Treasure Basket

Why is it good for your baby?

Babies are new to this world. They don't know that things made from wood feel and look different from shiny metal. When trying to lift a heavy object, they are surprised that it takes more effort. Babies are full of curiosity: they want to find out! Sat at a Treasure Basket a baby wants to reach out, touch, feel, pick up and explore the objects, and hold, smell and bang them. By mouthing, sucking, biting, licking she discovers textures, shapes, smell, taste and temperature. When all his senses are drawn into one focus of attention like that, his brain grows making lots of new connections and his mind develops ready for language. Your baby gains confidence, when allowed to explore alone and to make his own choices.It gives him great satisfaction and pleasure. Babies at a Treasure Basket will concentrate on exploring, observing and learning for a very long time, sometimes even up to 1 hour or longer.

A very well stocked Treasure Basket

Do babies have to put everything into their mouths?

Yes, because it is with their mouth that babies first make contact with the outside world. By sucking, mouthing and handling the baby finds out about weight, size, shape, taste, smell and sound. Mouthing objects helps a baby to move to the next developmental stage.

Every Treasure Basket is different

Babies must never be left alone with a Treasure Basket.

An adult needs to sit nearby and enjoy observing what the baby does. Let your baby choose! How does he do it? When the baby looks at your face to check that your mind and eyes are still on him, then he is talking to you, not yet with words but with his eyes. Sometimes he may need you to sit him up again.

So many things and textures to explore ...

'But won't my baby hurt himself?'

No, he won't. Not if you have checked the objects and are sitting nearby, watching and allowing him to explore as he can. Most of these worries belong to adults who have not paid close attention to how very careful babies are, when exploring new things around them. Small babies cannot throw things, and you are near enough to gently move his hand. Try not to pass your anxiety on to the baby. If you worry that he might swallow something, try swallowing it yourself: if you can't then he can't, as you are much bigger.

... and learn from their own experience of touching, sensing, feeling

How to look after a Treasure Basket

Safety and Hygiene are very important and to treat these 'learning-tools' with careful respect. All objects must be sorted and washed regularly, checked that there are no sharp edges and no lose bits that could come off. New objects must be added regularly. Older children must not be allowed to take things away from the basket.

What people say about Treasure Baskets:

Mother of Lenny (9 months): 'I never knew that he could do all those things. He's amazing! I want a Treasure Basket at my home now. I learnt so much just watching her, and I feel as if I saw my son in a new light today.'

Kylie + Ken's Parents (twins, 7 months): 'Thank you so much for organising this series of Treasure Basket sessions for us. It was great to meet at our house with the other mums and dads and babies every week. Discussing the videos and our observations taught us all so much about child development, about our babies, – and about ourselves. All our children now have a Treasure Basket. Each is different, – and definitely their favourite activity!'

What can you put in a Treasure Basket?

Any natural, household and real life objects made from different materials, but not plastic or toys designed by an adult with a purpose in mind, e.g.:

Natural Objects:	Everyday Objects:	Household Objects:	From the Kitchen	From the Bathroom
lemon	a bunch of keys	a shaving brush	egg whisk	flannel
avocado	small bell	shoe horn	small pan + lid	natural sponge
fir cones	coloured ribbon	wooden nail or	wooden + big	nail+body brush
smooth shells	curtain ring	other brushes	metal spoons	pumice stone
large pebbles	small glass bottle	clean duster-cloth	egg cup	loofah
natural sponge	paper-bag	small colourful	tea strainer	plug+chain
	wooden clothes pegs	scarf	bottle brush	
	small basket	a coaster	clean washing-	
	cotton reel		up brush +	
	leather-belt		scourer	
	glasses case			
	bag of herbs			
	smooth heavy glass			
	metal paper-weight			

To buy a Treasure Basket, or to arrange Treasure Basket sessions, consultancy or training, contact info@mindbuilders-consulting.org

Playing makes Babies' Brains Grow

Early Brain Development

The 'wiring' that happens during these early years from the baby's many 'first experiences' with the world, lays the foundation for all his/ her future experiences.

During the first months of life
→ Everything is a first experience.
→ A young child's brain and mind are growing and developing as fast as never again,
→ building complex structures and
→ laying foundations for all later learning that
→ enable his/her mind to think, feel and make sense of the world.

Babies actively try to make sense of their world ...

The Brain does Not Wait

→ Research shows that the foundation of the human brain is 'built' during the first 2 years of a baby's life.
→ After birth, a baby's brain 'builds' itself to fit the world that the child will live in through his/her social experiences with his/her parents/family.
→ Early interactions through playful talking, singing and 'mouth-and face-games' with mother/ parents/ carers directly affect the growth of a baby's brain.

Babies talk with their eyes and gestures. This baby is asking her brother: 'Come and play with me!

→ A baby's brain more than doubles its weight in the first year and most of its growth is done by age 3.
→ Early brain development is like 'an elaborate dance between biology and the environment' or between genes and the child's early experiences of interaction with his parents/ care-givers (Greenspan).
→ It is not a monologue of just putting food into the baby as if putting petrol into a car!
→ When a baby is not talked to and played with enough during the first year and left alone too much, then his/ her brain and mind do not grow and develop well, because
→ 'The brain feeds on experience, and without food (made from social play and experiences) the nervous system withers' (Hobson 2002) and dies because ...
→ THE BRAIN DOES NOT WAIT!

Babies communicating and observing each other while exploring a Treasure Basket.

Developmental Sequence of Basic Activities and Learning

Here is a list by Carol Mannion, a Developmental Therapist, of the developmental achievements a baby learns, and needs to learn, through interactions with his parents and his explorations of his environment in his first year:

→ **Grasping:** Holding own fingers and feet. Holding a portion of own clothes or tie ribbon. Holding another's finger or hand. Holding a rattle etc.

→ **Give and Take:** Taking an object from another person, giving and offering an object to another person.

→ **Reaching:** Working hard to reach an object that is just out of reach, getting it and then sending it out of reach again and again and again, with the reaching out hand. Puts arms out to a parent to be lifted up.

→ **Rolling over:** from lying on tummy to back, from back to front. This involves a lot of moving, effort and coordinating different parts of the body in order to achieve a goal. The baby is using his legs, feet, arms, hands, head and eyes, building up his confidence and sense of self, feeling 'I did it!' and 'I can do it!'

→ **IN and OUT**: Spending time sitting on the floor with a box or basket of objects, picking one out, licking, mouthing, and looking and handling it, and then putting it back in the basket and then selecting another object. This is an endless repetition that child does not tire of, and lasts for some weeks or months.

→ **Losing and Finding:** Object permanence and early separation sequence. The child is able to find his toy or blanket, if he sees you hide it under a cushion or so. Peek-a-boo games, where mum/dad hides under the cloth and reappears safely, or later the child's head can be covered and uncovered too, thus going away and coming back. Throwing things away/out of cot and wanting them to be brought back so that he can repeat the game. Playing a rhyme game like 'Under the Water' and being able to enjoy the sensation of going away and returning safely, for a few seconds.

→ **Curiosity:** The child looks for things, opens and closes cupboard doors, pulls things out, looks in handbags or boxes. Lifts things up to see what is underneath. Looks intently if you put on a mysterious voice and show him a box, and then rattle it, saying 'What's inside?' And then you slowly open the lid and show him.

ON and OFF: Putting the light switch on and off. Pulling off hat gloves, shoes, socks etc. Reaching up to a higher surface to take things, to put things on a table or chair.

Grasping and exploring his own body give the baby first experiences of his sense of self

Reaching out requires the baby to coordinate many different parts of his body

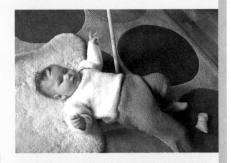

Rolling over is an important developmental achievement.

Pulling things off comes first. Putting balls on pegs, putting rings on posts. Replacing comes when 'off' is mastered.

→ **DOWN and UP:** Throwing things down to hear the noise or see the affect. Sliding objects down a slope or down the stairs. Putting things in and watching them go down, as through a clear tube. Putting things through a tube and awaiting their reappearance, out the other end. – Throwing a ball up a little and watching it come down. – Watching bubbles blown up in the air and trying to catch them as they come down. – Throwing feathers or light paper balls or sponge balls into the air. – In these activities the child is engaging more of his whole body and the eyes and ears.

Sitting without support enables the baby to use her hands, as well as her mouth, to explore the world

→ **POINTING and 'LOOK!'** Using the index finger to draw attention to something they have seen or want to show another person. The beginning of shared attention with intention.

→ **Feeling** what's **Outside:** The touching and feeling of objects, self, hair, mum, dad, food etc. – One can often observe the child fingering the labels on toys, blankets, raking the floor or carpet with tips of fingers. Very light touch and very hard touch, as if working out the possibilities of the texture. – Using the mouth tongue and lips to explore the texture, especially the squeeze and squeak toys. Biting with the gums and exploring with the tongue, so important to the development of muscles later needed for speech. – The pleasure of mouthing a hard object and the subsequent copious drooling and dribbling that accompanies the activity. – Dummy sucking prevents the child from doing this adequately and may be adding to the problem of speech delay in the early years.

Toddlers exploring the world around them: walking, bending, picking up, grasping, letting go ...

→ **Posting things:** Posting things into a slot and seeing them reappear. – Posting things into a can or box or money box. Rattling it. – Opening a drawer, closing it, opening, – then seeing things reappear. Repeating the process.

→ **Repetition:** At this stage of development, repetition is paramount for some time.

Pointing in order to show another person something they don't know yet is the beginning of wanting to talk

Some Modern Inventions do NOT help Babies' Development

A number of modern inventions do not help babies' development, because they run counter to the crucial 'use it or lose it' rule of early brain development by interfering with the fundamental natural processes for active exploration, learning from experience and the crucial place of loving interactions with other people as described above:

WARNING!

What to AVOID :
TV, video, baby-computers, mobiles, iPhones, battery-operated, electronic and press-the-button toys absorb the child's mind, making him quiet and passive, thus obstructing his active exploration of his environment. Where the TV is on all the time as 'sound-wallpaper', people talk less in families, resulting in increasing numbers of children arriving at nursery unable to speak, because they don't hear people talking enough at home. The American Association of Paediatricians strongly recommends that babies under the age of 2 years should watch NO television or videos, because of its negative affects on their brain development.

Mobile phone: if you are with your child, do you always give preference to your mobile by answering it, whenever this machine demands your attention? Imagine how being constantly interrupted in his interactions with you may feel to your child, and how this will become hard-wired in his brain.

Buggies facing out mean that all the time you are out, your baby is alone with his experiences and what he sees, i.e. he cannot read from your face, whether mummy thinks something he sees is dangerous or ok, and you cannot see or comment on, what your baby is seeing and feeling. Buggies or prams that face in allow the adult to observe their baby's face, to see what the baby is looking at and interested in, so the adult can comment on this and thus help their child connect what he sees with language. Just think how much time you could spend talking with your baby about what HE is interested in, if you were facing each other.

Baby walkers: Research shows that more babies get hurt and have accidents in baby walkers than when crawling or in a play-pen, e.g. rolling down the stairs, resulting in broken bones and head injuries, reaching high up, pulling down table cloths, getting burned and even poisoned. In Canada parents risk 6 months in jail for using a baby-walker. But what is worse is that baby-walkers ignore a baby's mental-emotional development, because they inhibit the child's crucial active movement explorations of using their arms and legs, stretching, rolling, scooting or crawling, and later pulling themselves upright. The result is that babies in baby-walkers learn to stand and walk later with other physical and mental-emotional delays (about 3 days of delay for every 24 hours of walker use).

Building Healthy Minds

Do you want to know more? Here some suggestions for further reading:

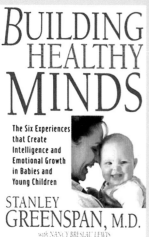

Building healthy minds: The Six Experiences That Create Intelligence and Emotional Growth in Babies and Young Children.

S. Greenspan with N. B. Lewis. Cambridge, MA: Perseus, 1999, ISBN-10: 0738203564

In this book Dr. Greenspan, a highly respected child psychiatrist, describes the 6 stages of development that are the foundation of intelligence and emotional growth in babies and young children.
   'Greenspan emphasizes that conversational and emotional exchanges between parents and infants are the basis for children's self-confidence, as well as their emotional and intellectual under-standings. He provides excellent recommendations for play time interactions, as well as pretend scenarios.' *Edythe Margolin*

Why Love Matters: How affection shapes a baby's brain

Sue Gerhard, 2004, Routledge, ISBN: 978-1-58391-817-3

'In 'Why love matters', Sue Gerhard, a psychotherapist, explains why love is essential to brain development in the early years of life, particularly to the development of our social and emotional brain systems, and presents the startling discoveries that provide the answers to how our emotional lives work. Sue Gerhardt considers how the earliest relationship shapes the baby's nervous system, with lasting consequences, and how our adult life is influenced by infancy despite our inability to remember babyhood. Why Love Matters is a lively and very accessible interpretation of the latest findings in neuroscience, psychology, psychoanalysis and biochemistry.'

How babies think: The science of childhood

Alison Gopnik, Patricia K Kuhl, Andrew Meltzoff, 2001, Phoenix, ISBN-10: 075381417X

'A fascinating look at how babies gain knowledge of the world and how much is actually ingrained from the day they are born. Using a massive range of research projects, the authors made an incredible range of discoveries, including that newborn babies know what their tongue looks like, that one-year-olds know the difference between Swedish and English and that 18-month-olds understand that some people prefer broccoli to crackers. It's not the easiest read – inevitably a book written by three professors can slip into too much analysis for the lay person. But it is detailed, fascinating and a refreshing look at how much your tot actually knows.'

When Things go Wrong:
Early Signs of Alarm

However, if things don't go too well at this early age, there can be dramatic consequences and recent research suggests that failure in early interactive play may play a part in a number of developmental disturbances. Babies who find their mother's face repeatedly blank and unresponsive to their invitation to play or smile, perhaps because she is withdrawn, preoccupied or depressed, will keep trying to reach her or to make her smile.

Some babies develop great skill and tenacity here, and do succeed in helping their mother overcome her depression, while others are less forceful or more sensitive and easily discouraged. Some babies who repeatedly fail to establish a satisfying communication with their mother eventually give up trying, becoming first confused then despondent, withdrawn and eventually depressed themselves.

The baby needs to come to trust that what he does, like averting his eyes, which is how he tells us how he feels, is understood and is successful in changing things he does not like and giving him the sense that he has some control over making himself feel better. The baby needs to develop a sense that he can make things happen in the world, that he can have a 'say' on what happens.

If self-regulatory behaviours like looking away or turning his head away, are not respected by the adult or are interfered with, then the baby might get scared and give up on people, as they do not respond in a helpful way, and he might no longer show how he feels in his face.

Worse still, he may come to associate the face-to-face position and eye-contact with an anxiety-provoking experience he can't cope with and will therefore avoid at all cost, which is one of the main features of autism.

Mark's mother felt terrible because 'He never looks at me. I call his name, but he doesn't look at me!' she complained. I suggested to 'Don't keep calling his name. Just smile at him, whenever you catch one of his fleeting glances at you.' When I met her again 6 months later, she told me that Mark's gaze-aversion had improved greatly and she felt much happier with their relationship with each other. Mark is now 6 years old and happily goes to main stream school. He likes to play with his brother, and his mum's only complaint is that he never stops talking.

This baby looks unhappy. Being immobilized in his mother's capuce all day makes him quiet. But it is only loving interactions and active exploration of his world that will make him happy

A baby who is not responding or avoiding eye contact with his mother, may find the approach intrusive and tries to protect himself from being overwhelmed

Why Early Intervention is so Important: Use it or Lose it!

→ Early development requires sensitive interactions and communication with adults for the baby's brain to grow under the main rule of early brain development, which is: 'USE IT OR LOSE IT!'

→ Especially during the first 2 years of life, there are what scientists call 'Sensitive Periods' or 'Windows of Opportunity' that open and close relatively quickly.

→ During these 'sensitive periods' babies must have enough opportunity to explore their own body, relationships with other people and the world around them for their brain to develop normally.

→ Without enough daily experiences of social interactions, being talked to and played with, the circuits and brain-connections of a baby's brain can not be put together properly with worrying consequences for the baby's emotional, social or cognitive intelligence.

→ Therefore, the earlier we can give attention to a young child's developmental and relationship problems, the better our chances for good progress.

Especially during the first 2 years of life, there are 'Sensitive Periods' or 'Windows of Opportunity' for certain fundamental learning, that open and close relatively quickly

SOME OBSTACLES TO EARLY DEVELOPMENT CAN HAVE LASTING EFFECTS
because a young child's:
→ brain is still growing
→ mind is not fully formed yet
→ relationships are still forming
→ behaviour patterns are not entrenched and can change much more easily than later on

Pre-autistic Warning Signs: Babies with Play and Relationship Problems

International research (from France, Germany, Israel, Italy, UK, USA) indicates that autism develops in the first 2 years of life and that it can often be treated successfully during this time. In Normandy in France, Prof. D. Houzel and Dr. P. Delion, began training health-professionals to recognise the early signs of autism in order to treat 'babies at risk of autism' or 'babies with relationship problems' before the age of 1 year. They found that parents reported concerns about their babies most frequently at birth and then at 5, 9, 18 and 24 months. But if parents' concerns was ignored during the baby's first year, then parents usually waited until the child

Small early obstructions can have lasting consequences: this tree started off straight and it would have grown up straight. But there was a wire fence in its way and because it grew through it, it now has a deformed trunk. If only someone had moved the wire out of the path of its growth early on (= early intervention)! Then this would now be a tree as well-formed as all the others. It's the same for all growth, – but especially that of a baby's brain

was 26 months before seeking advice again, thus losing out on the most vital time to influence brain-development. Stella Acquarone and in 1990, Hisako Watanabe from Japan, were pioneers in the UK in discussing the treatment of early signs of autism, based on intersubjectivity, communication, posture and sensory difficulties. In Paris in 1998, Prof. Graciella Crespin, M.C Laznik and others founded 'Association Pre-Aut' for the prevention of autism in France.

Arising as a result of a combination of biological, neurological and other maturational processes in early brain and psychological development, developmental problems follow the 'use it or lose it' rule. These fundamental early processes are 'use-dependent' on the psycho-biochemical regulation in a nurturing and stimulating social environment (Balbernie 2002), i.e. on sensitive and attuned interactions with the child's main relationships (Sunderland 2002).

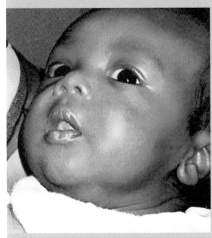

A baby who spends a lot of time avoiding emotional contact may give cause for concern, – if this happens every day and continues for several weeks

The importance of intervening as early as possible:

A 6-month-old found to have breathing or kidney problems will receive medical attention and help immediately, because it
→ *is better to have false positives*
→ *will be cheaper to intervene as early as possible*
→ *might be life-saving*

But with mental/ psychological problems like autism
→ *there is a multi-stranded route*
→ *that takes a long time, and involves much waiting*
→ *starting too late*
→ *not taking the early concerns sufficiently seriously*
→ *thus often missing the crucial windows or opportunities for prevention*

But as recent research shows, the brain of a baby has an enormous capacity for growth and change during the first 2 years of life. This means that in the case of developmental difficulties, the earlier intervention begins the greater the chances to redirect development onto a more healthy or 'normal' course. See also www.mifne-autism.com.

→ Babies with **pre-autistic** warning signs may be able to recover, when parents get appropriate therapeutic help in the first year.
→ 'If you want to prevent crystallisation of autism, you have to dispel this atmosphere of doom and gloom, and introduce joy and musical interaction.' (Trevarthen 2005)

Hand-waving can be a form of self-comforting

Pre-autistic warning signs in babies under 12 months include:
1. Relationship and Sensory Difficulties
2. Posture, Tonicity and Motor Development
3. Pre-linguistic Communication Problems
4. Eating/ Feeding Problems
5. Behavioural Problems

Founded by Hanna Alonim in 1987, an expert in early child-hood development disorders of the autism spectrum in Israel, the Mifne-Centre ('Turning-point') works with families of babies and young autistic children with a surprisingly high success rate. '**Where parents are actively involved** in working and engaging with their autistic child during the first 3 years, we achieve **unexpectedly good results**.' (Alonim 2002)

Problems with posture, tonicity and motor development, such as being floppy, can be early warning signs

Signs of Pre-Autism:
adapted from 'ESPASI – Early Signs of Pre-Autism Scale for Infants' by Hanna Alonim 2004, Mifne Centre, Israel. See www.mifne-autism.com

1. **Unusually passive**: *baby never cries and shows no interest in the world around him/ her*
2. **Unusually active:** *baby cries all the time and never seems to be able to calm down*
3. **Feeding problems:** *baby refuses or is resistant to feed from breast, bottle or spoon*
4. **Unresponsive:** *baby does not react to the parent's voice or presence, does not look, smile, turn his head or babble in response to his parent/carers*
5. **Tactile aversions:** *baby is not comforted by being held and does not like to be touched by anybody*
6. **No eye-contact:** *baby avoids direct eye-contact with people, but looks at objects*
7. **Movement problems:** *baby's movements or muscle tone are unusually flaccid or stiff*

Feeding problems are a sign of relationship problems, that need thoughtful attention

IMPORTANT!
→ *At least 3 of these early signs must have been consistently present over a period of at least 3 weeks.*
→ *A complete physical examination should always be the first step in the diagnostic process.*
→ *Assessment of pre-autistic warning signs requires guidance from an appropriately trained specialist.*

Early Signs of ASD in Infants and Young Children

Foundations for Relating, Communication and Thinking	Early Signs of Core Deficits of ASD	Associated Symptoms
Shared attention and regulation (begins at 0-3 months) Calm interest in and purposeful responses to sights, sound, touch, movement, and other sensory experiences (e.g., looking, turning to sounds)	Lack of sustained attention to different sights or sounds	Aimless or self-stimulatory behaviour
Engagement and relating (begins at 2-5 months)) Growing expression of intimacy and relatedness (e.g., a gleam in the eye and joyful smiles initiated and sustained)	No engagement or only fleeting expression of joy, rather then robust, sustained engagement	Self-absorption or withdrawal
Purposeful emotional interactions (begins at 4-10 months) A range of back-and-forth interactions, with emotional expressions, sounds, hand gestures, and the like used to convey intentions	No interactions or only brief back-and-forth interactions with little initiative (i.e., mostly responding)	Unpredictable (random or impulsive) behaviour
Long chains of back-and-forth emotional signaling and shared problem-solving (e.g. joint attention) (begins at 10-18 months) Many social and emotional interactions in a row used for problem-solving (e.g., showing Dad a toy)	Inability to initiate and sustain many consecutive back-and-forth social interactions or exchanges of emotional signals	Repetitive or perseverative behaviour
Creating ideas (begins at 18-30 months) Meaningful use of words or phrases and interactive pretend play with caregivers or peers	No words, or rote use of words (e.g., mostly repeats what is heard)	Echolalia and other forms of repetition of what's heard or seen
Building bridges between ideas: logical thinking (begins at 30-42 months) Logical connections between meaningful ideas ('Want to go outside *because* I want to play')	No words, or memorised scripts, coupled with seemingly random, rather than logical, use of ideas	Irrational behaviour or illogical or unrealistic use of ideas

Engaging Autism, By S. Greenspan and S. Wieder, Da Capo Book.

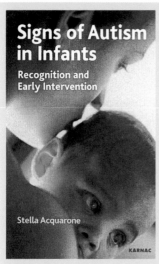

Signs of autism in infants: Recognition and early intervention

Edited: Stella Acquarone, 2007, Karnac,
ISBN 9781855754867

The contributors to this book focus on the possibility of preventing the full development of autistic behaviour, identifying early signs of alarm and a model of psychoanalytically informed interventions to treat the pre-autistic infant. ... autism has been identified as a developmental impairment due to a variety of causes which may include genetic, neurological, infectious, metabolic, immunologic and environmental factors, all contributing to atypical brain development, which in turn leads to the autistic child's 'deficient experience of intersubjectivity', as Peter Hobson has defined it. Neonatal research reveals that innate capacities for sociability, self-regulation, thought and language are activated through intensely bi-directional emotional interactions with others, within critical periods. Neonatal research also confirms that even genetic endowment is modified or inhibited by the specific emotional climate of the family environment into which each baby is born. Although the prevention of autism still lies in the future, this book offers hope of alleviating distress through psychodynamic therapeutic work with the family to enhance intersubjective communication and foster the growth potential of the infant.

Stories of Successful Early Intervention

The Boy who Loved Windows

Soon after his birth, his mother had noticed an emptiness in his gaze – a vacant quality that emphasized her sense that he was ill at ease in his own body. By the time Walker was five months old, his gaze was obsessively directed towards windows – light had become his true north.

When Walker, 'the boy who loved windows', was 6 months his parents were told that he would never walk or talk, or even hear or see because of 'sensory integration problems', a term inextricably linked with autism.

Unwilling to accept this grim prognosis, his parents spent the next 5 years working with him all day, 'to bring him into full contact with the world'.

'A baby's development is like building a house' says his mother, Patricia Stacey, describing how they spent 5 years 're-building' his mind and brain in hours of hard work, Now Walker is 5 and talks and plays like other children.

A Boy Beyond Reach

Dr. Cheri Florance, describes in 'A Boy Beyond Reach' and 'The Maverick Mind: A Mother's Story of Solving the Mystery of Her Unreachable, Untouchable, Silent Son' Whitney's mother, how

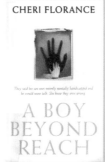

she discovered how to teach her son to communicate in more conventional ways and to excel in school, sports and life by using pictures despite opposition from doctors, teachers, and psychologists.

Graham's Story: Autistic-like. When it's not autism. What is it? (Audio CD)

'When their son was just 17 months old, Erik and Jennie Linthorst suspected something was not quite right. Experts and therapists told them their son was autistic. Sort of. Maybe. Some called him autistic-like. Others said he was not autistic at all. With his parents still seeking a clear diagnosis, Graham was launched into a programme of behavioural therapy. Speech therapy. Occupational therapy. Soon after the therapy began, Erik and Jennie noticed something else: the treatment he was getting didn't seem to be on target. Erik took on the conundrum confronting many parents of kids who are 'mildly disordered'. Handed a fuzzy diagnosis, what should the treatment be?

Autistic-like is an intimate family portrait showing one dad's determined quest to find the right therapies, the right doctors, and even the right words to describe his son. As he searched, Eric began wondering how other families in the same situation fare. What did it really mean, 'autistic-like'? And how should or could these parents help their kids? The CD says one in every 100 children born in the US has autism. Maybe not.' See:
www.autisticlike.com

Isaac: A Mother's Journey to discover her Baby

'Dear Health-visitor, I just wanted to let you know, how Isaac is getting on. He is almost 18 months now. It's been quite a journey. But things are going well and I'm now not worried about autism any more, because I feel I'm in such good emotional contact with Isaac. We understand each other. We love being together. He shows me things by pointing and then checking my face to see my response. He starts interactive games. He surprises me with new ideas. He even teases me. Yesterday he offered me some of his apple, but then kept feeding it to his teddy, with this twinkle in his eye that just made me laugh. He talks using gestures and I understand what he means with his gestures. I have slowed down to so much. I try to get onto his level and understand him from his point of view. We have so much fun together. And most of the time it is Isaac who starts it. Or he tries to help me by crawling off to bring me my shoes or my keys ...

I really don't know, where things started to go wrong. Everything was fine, when Isaac was born, even though he wasn't planned. He was a big surprise. But he was such an easy baby. He was happy in his crib for hours. He loved the TV.

I took him to baby groups every week. It was there that I first got worried. He didn't join in like the other babies. He didn't look around like they did. I thought, if I took him more often and let him watch more of the clever-baby videos, it would help. I tried really hard. But he basically stopped making eye contact altogether. I think he was about 7 or 8 months then. I was beside myself, searching for help.

The baby massage group you sent me to really helped. He loved it and it helped me to slow down. I now also understand that the rhythm of the massage movements helped both him and me to get into more of a dialogue, and he started to relax and make eye contact again.

But it was the home-consultations by the early interventionist you referred me to, that really changed everything. She came to observe and helped me to think about what might be going on in Isaac's mind. She helped me to understand how communication develops and how rhythm and daily routines help with that. We didn't have any routines then. I just used to fit in with Issac. I realised how important predictable daily routines are, because they are like a language that tell the baby what is going to happen and in what order.

We talked about different sensory profiles of different babies. We observed that Isaac is a bit slow and needs more time to process what is going on. The first thing I realised was that I was doing too much. I just didn't give him a chance to respond. I had to wait a bit longer. Then he would respond. It was as if he was still asleep and needed waking up to become more interested in the world. Sometimes he did something different than I had expected. It took me a while not to be upset by that. I used to feel that I had failed to teach him properly, if he did things differently. Now I realise that babies have their own ideas, already at this young age. I realised that he was already a complete person. I really used to think that it was my job to make him into a person. I really thought that being a good mum was about keeping him safe and making him happy, and then he would become a person one day. It was a bit of a shock to realise it's a two-way thing, that we need to do this together. It wasn't easy and I went through lots of ups and downs about it all. Without the support from the early intervention therapist I would not have managed to make those fundamental changes.

With her help, I became interested in Isaac in a different way. I became curious to find out, who this small person is. I wanted to discover him. I listened more. And I listened differently. I stopped listening just whether he was unhappy and rushing to make him happy again. And I stopped feeling guilty all the time that I wasn't a good mum every time he wasn't happy. Instead I began to watch and listen to what he was thinking, to his ideas, to what he was telling me with his body language and facial expressions, to what HE was interested in. His favourite game was making things disappear. He'd push things under the sofa cushions and then he'd look at me waiting for me to say 'Oops. It's gone!?' Then he'd pull the toy out again with a big grin saying 'daah'. He loved peekaboo and started to surprise me with his 'booh!'s. It was so funny. That's when I realised, we were going to be ok. Oh, and I've stopped the TV and videos, and going to those groups. We have more fun playing together at home. I hope you don't mind? Thank you so much for listening to me, and for getting us those home consultations.'

(All names and other identifying details have been changed.)

Lucy: Finding her Place in the World

Lucy was a bit of a surprise. Her mum was breastfeeding her brother, who was not yet 1 when Lucy was born, and hadn't even thought of other babies. But Lucy did and decided to come anyway and whatever it took. It was just before Christmas, when she'd had enough and wanted out. It was not her time yet, when 'She literally jumped into my hands', said her dad. Lucy was not only premature. She also got ill and had to spend weeks in Intensive Care. When she got home, she screamed. Nothing seemed to help. Carrying her was wrong. Putting her down was wrong. Talking was wrong. Singing was wrong. And she was somehow stiff, when someone held her. Except her mum. She didn't mould comfortably to the other person like babies normally do. Except her mum. It was as if she couldn't really let herself be held, as if she had to hold herself. Except her mum. One evening Lucy had woken up. She was about 8 months. Her dad was holding her and tried to talk to her. But Lucy would not look at him. Not at all. She'd avert her eyes, turn her head, move her body away. It was very painful to watch.

But her mum was not worried. She could see the problem. But she was going to pull this kid out of any self-absorbed or difficult mental spaces. She carried on coaxing Lucy into little games, included her with her little brother, gave her time to respond and predictable routines to hold on to. Her brother also helped, – with his love, his jealousy, his showing her what he could do. And Lucy would practice with incredible patience, until she could 'do it too'. Once Lucy could crawl, the screaming stopped. It was as if she was desperate to move around. Her mum devoted herself completely to helping her 2 babies play without getting into fights. She would sit between them, protect what each was playing with like traffic police, and interact with each on their developmental level. In this way they could see and watch each other, while safe to explore their world in their own ways. In this way, Lucy and her brother became best friends, – once she got out of the age of trying to knock down his towers all the time. It was as if it was only then, that Lucy found her place in the world.

Now Lucy is 5 and a confident, and sometimes stroppy, little girl who can hold her own towards her bossy brother. She is creative, sociable and a great story teller. Sometimes lies too, if it gets her out of trouble. She is a bit clumsy and not as agile as her brother, who cannot ever tell a lie. Lucy loves nursery, where she has lots of friends, and has learnt to read before her older brother. And she loves everything that is pink, because that's her favourite colour.

(All names and other identifying details have been changed.)

Habib: Can Traumatic Experiences as a Baby be linked to Autistic Behaviours?

Habib was born with a heart-defect. Aged 3 months, he was in intensive care for weeks after the operation. His babyhood was overshadowed by his father's violence towards his mother and abusive relationship with Habib and his older brother.

When I met Habib, he seemed to spend most of his time with his head on the floor crawling round and round the room in circles. He did not talk. He did not play. And there wasn't much to play with. He was 3 years old. Habib's mum had left her abusive husband and had moved back to her mum. They had tried to teach Habib to 'sit properly'. It made him crawl in circles even more. He'd scream when anyone tried to stop him. And then he'd crawl off with his head on the floor again. Mum went to seek help. She got a diagnosis. Autism. What's that? Did it matter? Could he improve, – get better? I said 'Who knows? Let's try.' We played. Mum got onto the floor and mirrored Habib crawling around the room. Habib stopped to look. He couldn't believe his eyes. He crawled on. Mum followed like a shadow. He could feel his mum do, what he did and felt. Amazing! He loved it. That's how it all started to change. They stopped trying to stop him. Mum mirrored him instead, – his crawling, his movements, his sounds. It didn't take long and the crawling stopped. There were ups and downs and new challenges. We got some recycling things as play materials and symbolic toys for the children to play with. Mum got some help for Habib's brother, who had been severely traumatised by the father's neglect and abuse.

When Habib was 5½ , mum complained about a new problem: 'I don't know what to do. He is talking non stop all the time! Constantly asking me questions. It is driving me crazy.' Often she did not know the answers. 'Mum, mum! Where is that girl going? Who threw that rubbish on the street? Who does the blue car over there belong to?' We talked about helping Habib to think for himself and to trust in his own mind: 'I don't know. What do you think, Habib?' One day they bumped into his dad in the street: 'Why did you hit my mum?', demanded Habib. Later his brother said to him 'Why didn't you say it in Bengali? Then he would've understood.' (as their dad doesn't speak English.)

Now 8 years old, Habib can read and write and loves to go to school, where he is popular and has a best friend. He attends class 3 of a mainstream school, but in English he attends year 4 as he is too advanced for his age-group. His mum now works as a support worker with other families with an autistic child coaching parents to play and teaching them what she learnt herself.
(All names and other identifying details have been changed.)

Maya: The Girl who had to 'Hold on Tight'

Maya was very ill when she was born and had to stay in intensive care for many weeks. Her own mum was not well enough to look after her, so her grandmother took the baby home to look after her. Granny loved Maya. From around 18 months the family started to worry. Maya did not talk at all. She did not play like other children her age, although she had some interest in her teddies, – making them walk, putting them to sleep. But it was impossible to join her in her play, because all she wanted to do was to hold on to whatever she had in her hand. Her gran carried her most of the time. She would then pick her up to comfort her, and let her have whatever she wanted. And she did not pooh. Often not for days or even weeks. Whenever Maya got frustrated, especially when she could not have or keep something she wanted, she would throw herself on the floor and scream and scream. It was terrible. The local diagnostic team said that Maya was autistic.

The family asked me to help. Gradually we worked out that although this made Maya go quiet, picking her up every time was actually not helpful. Nor was it helpful to carry her so much or do everything for her, as she was no longer a tiny baby. Instead, Maya needed more encouragement to be independent and to have fun with other people.

By now Maya's mum had recovered and came to visit every day. Maya loved climbing on her lap. Gran, mum, Maya and I worked together for about 1 year, trying to understand what was going on, how to woo Maya into wanting to play with us and to help her build her mind. Eventually Maya started nursery. Gran didn't think she'd manage. Maya loved it. At nursery Maya got so busy playing, that she forgot about holding on to things, including her pooh.

A year later I met Maya and her family again. They wanted to share that Maya is now talking and playing like any other child. That even school can't see anything different about this little girl. Maya is keen to learn and popular with other children. She has lots of friends. 'Mummy, mummy, can you help me climb up over there!', called Maya as I was talking to her mum for too long.
(All names and other identifying details have been changed.)

Shahida and her Autistic Brother Abdul:
'It's genetic, innit?' or The Complex Relationship between Genetics and Environment.

Shahida was a few months old, when her 3 year old brother Abdul was diagnosed as autistic. Mum was devastated. Dad did not know what to do. Parents did not understand. Their English was not very good, so they could not read the leaflets they were given, or find out more from books or websites. When I first visited to support the family through home consultations with Abdul, it was chaos. Parents were frantically trying to 'teach' their son to be 'normal', resulting in lots of screaming and increased puzzling and difficult behaviours.

There was no time or attention left for Shahida, who was left on the settee, in front of the TV or carried around like a bag, while parents were trying to make Abdul do things he did not want or know how to do. At 9 months Shahida was sent to a nursery full time by the local authority. By 15 months, she was walking, eating and sleeping alright. But otherwise she sorted herself out, making no demands on other people for attention or interaction. She did not play. She did not point. She made little eye contact and did not reference other people. She did not vocalise or try to talk. The nursery became concerned. Staff talked about autism. 'It's genetic, innit?', they said, 'and her brother's got it, innit?', they said, obviously unaware of the incredibly complex nature-nurture inter-relationship between genetics and environment, especially when it comes to the huge developmental potential of a baby's growing mind and brain.

Mum called me to come and see Shahida. We talked about what little children need to develop their personality and communication skills. I explained that babies and little children need time and attention from adults who are interested in the child's mind. In order to become interested in talking and communicating, a baby needs someone who enjoys talking and playing with her, with TV and all other electronics switched off, and with opportunities to explore the world around them (as described throughout this book).

Things changed. The TV was off most of the time. Mum gave more attention to Shahida. She stopped just handing her the bottle to drink by herself and talked more with her. Dad made time to play with Shahida every day (he is the better player of the parents). By now we had sorted out a routine for Abdul. Parents were more confident. Abdul had begun to interact more with his family. He had become more interested in communication. He started to use some words. His behaviour problems were mostly gone, though he slept late. So parents made time to play with him for 2 hours every evening, when his sisters were asleep.

By the age of 2½ Shahida started to talk. But she was very attention seeking and jealous of her brother getting attention. Parents worried, until I explained that this was a good thing: it was as if Shahida was hungry for the kind of interested attention she didn't have enough of, when she was a baby.

Now Shahida is 6 and never stops talking. She has many friends at school, where she is ahead in reading and writing. If anyone said that she was once considered as possibly autistic, people would not believe it, or laugh at the joke.

Abdul too has made fantastic progress. He talks and argues with his sisters, especially Shahida, and complains to mum that 'Shahida keeps teasing me! Tell her to stop it.' He too can read and write, attends a football club, is popular at school, and parents are happy with his development. Mum's only concern is that Abdul only likes chicken curry, but not meat or fish. 'Is that your only problem?', I asked in disbelief. 'Yes.', she said. *(All names and other identifying details have been changed.)*

3 Playing in the family

Getting ready to Play:
Who is Who in the Family?

A family is a social unit traditionally forming a household or inhabiting a home, whose members are related to each other, though not necessarily biologically. Modern families are often very different from families in the past, and they come in many different shapes and sizes and including different members: mothers, fathers, children, grand-parents, aunts, uncles, cousins, step-, foster, surrogate, and adopted children/parents, ... There are extended families with members from several generations, and nuclear families consisting of only parent/s and child/ren. In 2010 about 25% of all families in the UK were single-parent families.

But families all over the world are made up of ADULTS and CHILDREN. And adults and children have different roles, different needs and different responsibilities to each other.

Drawing by a 9 year old of her family: 2 'big' children, mum holding the tiny new baby, and dad

The Adults' job is to provide
1. the material resources and money to pay for what the family needs, e.g. food, clothes, warmth, protection and a home, i.e. a safe space for the children to live, sleep, eat, play and to GROW UP in
2. the mental-emotional support needed to BRING UP a child so he can build his mind, i.e. love and emotional warmth, understanding, interest and attention, encouragement, guidance and clear boundaries ...

Children need careful guidance from their parents in order to grow up well

What about the Children?
→ A child's main job is to PLAY, because this is how children learn about themselves and the world they live in.
→ Sometimes people say 'Oh, it's just a baby!' But 'There is no such thing as a baby', because a human baby can only live and survive with someone looking after him/her.
→ A child's early relationships with his parents at home create the blue-print inside the child's mind that he will use for all other relationships.
→ Children don't just grow up 'automatically' like the young of many animals, because the human brain is in fact built through the interactive regulation at home with the child's mother/primary carer, especially during the first 2-3 years.
→ Children need parents/carers to bring them up and to give them lots of time, love and attention. Just food, clothes, a place to sleep, lots of toys and school are not enough.
→ In fact, a child is only 'on loan' to his parents, – until he is grown up enough to become 'his own person'.

Playing is a child's work and way of talking

Parenting:
The Hardest Job on Earth

BECOMING a parent: 'It's so easily done!'
Becoming pregnant and having a baby is the easy part.
But BEING a parent is the hardest thing you'll ever do!

Children don't come with instructions, and parenting is a continuous process of trial and error.

What is a Parent's Job?

What is a parent's job?
a) to make the child happy?
b) to help the child make her/himself happy?

A parent's job includes not only the basic physical care of giving their child healthy food to eat, sensible clothes to wear, a place to sleep and a family to belong to.

A child who has all of this and perhaps even lots of toys, TV and expensive things, will suffer neglect with serious consequences for his/her brain and mental development, if s/he does not also have enough of his/her parent's time, love, interest and attention, as well as shared play.

In order to develop well a young child needs from his parents:
→ emotional and spiritual nurturing
→ attuned attention to his/her emotional needs
→ the awareness that children already have their own ideas in their minds
→ being talked and listened to like an equal partner from birth onwards
→ social play and playful interaction with his main carers/ parents and other family members and friends
→ stimulation, e.g. suitable toys and play-materials to explore and play with
→ sufficient space to play, so he can explore and learn how the world works
→ structure in the environment, e.g. storage/shelves, so he can tidy up and find his toys and play-things
→ daily routines, boundaries and family-rules, so he can build up a sense of the rhythm of time
→ attention to his/her individual needs, strengths and weaknesses
→ guidance and age-appropriate challenges that help the child to learn from his own experiences

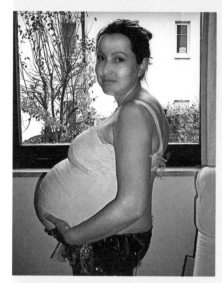
Getting pregnant and having a baby: that's the easy bit

A dad's photo of the first child's awe and wonder at the miracle of a new baby

Parents/Carers Need to help their Child to

1. **BUILD his/her MIND**, i.e. to use their mind for thinking, to use their imagination, to be able to solve problems creatively and to think for themselves
2. **REGULATE him/herself** and to **manage his/her FEELINGS**, especially 'bad', painful, frightening and overwhelming feelings of 'too much'-ness, e.g. anger, frustration, sadness, excitement, loss, …
3. **generate LOVE**, i.e. to feel loved and loveable, to enjoy being with other people and to be considerate of other people's feelings
4. **have HOPE for the future**, i.e. to have aims and aspirations, and not to give in to depressive feelings

This boy has everything. But he is unhappy

Self-regulation and Parents: Regulators or Dys-regulators?

A crucial part of a parent's job is to help their child to regulate himself, i.e. to find ways to calm himself down, when he is too excited, and to manage painful feelings such as frustration, anger, sadness, jealousy, etc. without lashing out or falling apart in a tantrum of rage, despair or panic. Without being able to manage their feelings, attention and impulses, a child cannot play and learn in peace.

Emotional regulation means helping your child to

1. develop their positive affect and feelings, i.e. feeling good about themselves and others
2. controlling their negative affect and manage their 'bad' feeling

His mother is trying to make her son happy by buying him lots of things, but he is still unhappy

THE BIGGEST QUESTIONS AS A PARENT ARE:
→ 'Am I a Regulator or a Dys-Regulator for my Child?'
→ 'Does the child feel better or worse, when they are with their parent/carer?'

If being with mum/dad makes a child feel worse, then the parent is not helping him to regulate, but is a 'dys-regulator'. The child will then experience the parent as a 'scare-giver' (Acquarone) rather than a 'care-giver', and suffer mental-emotional pain. He might even cut off, withdraw and stop communicating or wanting to be with people.

If you think you are a 'dys-regulator' don't despair. Occasional dys-regulation is completely normal, and just paying attention to being more regulating will help. Or find someone to talk to about it, like a psychologist or psychotherapist.

Now the boy is happy. He did not want things. He wanted his mum to be interested, to listen, talk and play with him

Dealing with Difficult Feelings

Human beings have lots of feelings all the time, good feelings and bad feelings. We wouldn't be human without them.
Everybody finds difficult or 'bad' feelings hard to deal with.
But we cannot just switch off or control our feelings just using
our will-power. Feelings and emotions have a way of their
own. They come and go, sometimes suddenly, sometimes
even flooding and overwhelming us with their forceful impact.
This is even more so for babies and children, who have little
experience yet. Children learn how to manage and survive
their strong feelings in the family and from their parents. They
learn from the way their parents help them to manage difficult
feelings, through supportive and thoughtful relationships.

Dealing with bad feelings is difficult, because
it is painful. But not impossible

   Telling a child to be quiet, or not to have these painful
feelings, or to pull themselves together, does not help a child
to learn how to regulate himself and how to manage himself
when feeling 'bad' in himself. In fact it will make a bad situation worse. If you are upset and someone tells you to be quiet,
to stop 'being silly' and to stop feeling upset: does this stop
you feeling upset? Most people would feel even more upset,
and now also angry. Upset feelings need interested attention
and UNDERSTANDING in order to calm down.

   When a child is genuinely upset, it is not the parent's job
to just stop the noise or the crying. That won't make it better.
Instead we need to try to understand the child's difficult feelings. He needs us to think about the situation and to find ways
to support him to manage his difficult feelings.

When parents help the child to manage their
difficult feelings, children learn to do so by
themselves. Upset feelings need interested
attention and understanding in order to calm
down

Children need help, guidance and understanding to manage
strong difficult feelings of frustration, anger, rage, jealousy,
envy, fear, over-excitement, and sometimes even hatred.
Helping a child to manage their difficult strong feelings means
being understanding, calm and containing. Telling him to 'stop
it!' or not to feel his feelings is not helping your child, but
making him feel even worse.

Adults can help by being calm and naming the feelings, e.g.:
'I understand that you are angry. But I cannot let you hurt me
or yourself or destroy things. I will hold you until you calm
down.' Or 'I will sit with you quietly on this chair until you calm
down and I am here if you need a cuddle.'

The idea of 'Containment'

In a mental process of 'Russian dolls', we aim to contain the
anxious impulse to 'do' something, when confronted with a
child's challenging behaviours, perhaps by using imagery to
encourage the process of generating 'dream-thoughts', that
can lead us to being able to think about what is going on and
what would be the best ways in which we can respond to the
difficult emotional situation.

Difficult feelings need to be contained and
put together in the mind like Russian dolls

Making Thinking Imaginable!

In order to be able to solve a problem one needs to be able to 'catch' one's thoughts into images, and then words and ideas that can be used for thinking and talking, thus 'making thinking imaginable.' It is a bit like the experience of waking with the sense of having had a dream without being able to remember any pictures, which then makes it impossible to think or talk about it, – and sometimes an uncomfortable sense follows us throughout the day like an invisible mental smell. Once we can talk about it, the words act as a container for those feelings that would otherwise remain uncontainable, unthinkable and causing confusion. This is what often happens to children and where they need our thoughtful attention and interest.

What is Behaviour?

Human behaviour is complex and fundamentally different from mechanical and simple cause-effect processes, because human behaviour always involves feelings and interactive/environmental elements.

The child's behaviour is his language

Behaviour is really a 'translation' of what is going on inside someone's mind into bodily expression, action and movement. Difficult feelings often lead to difficult behaviours, because difficult feelings are difficult to tolerate and manage.

Behaviour difficulties: Whose behaviour?

Behaviour difficulties are a communication of difficult and painful emotional states of mind, i.e. of 'feeling bad', using actions and 'doing things' instead of using one's mind for thinking and putting our thoughts and feelings into words.

The problem is not the behaviour, but to find out and understand what is going on:
What is this behaviour saying and what is it a response to? What is behind this behaviour, what is it about?

Sometimes the problem is not only the child's 'behaviour difficulties', but also difficult behaviours in parents. Sometimes parents don't realise, they too are making things more difficult. Sometimes they too feel 'bad', confused and helpless. It is difficult to think, when one is feeling 'bad'. Unable to think their way out of their problem, the adult ends up feeling trapped, – and unable to think clearly, just like the child with the difficult behaviours.

However, it is at the very point, when we realise that we have a problem that we are beginning to be able to find a way out of our dilemma by thinking about it and towards solving 'the problem'. The adult needs to be able to think and use

Behind every behaviour is a positive intention.

This girl needs to get out and move her body! She's been indoors all day. But her mum shouts that she hasn't got time. That makes the girl want to get out even more! It 'dys-regulates' the child rather than helping her to manage her difficult feelings

Here mum helps her child to regulate her feelings by explaining the plan of the day: 'FIRST ... THEN ...'. This helps the child to structure and build her mind, to learn to wait and to think ahead

their own mental-emotional resources in order to solve their child's behaviour problems, rather than 'blaming' difficult feelings on the child or on others.

The boy is standing on the table looking down on his dad telling him to get off. What might this behaviour be about?

Mum is trying to deal with the problem and jumps up, when she sees the child climb onto the table again

How to cope with difficult behaviours?

→ Keep the presenting 'behaviour problem' in mind, but

→ Do NOT focus on just wanting to change/stop the unwanted behaviour. If you do, you will end up in a battle of wills with each side feeling misunderstood and angry.

→ Instead: comment, observe and continue to be interested in 'What is going on inside the child's mind?'

→ Try to clarify confusions, e.g. the child does not understand that jumping off the table is NOT a game and that his parents will NOT allow it.

→ Don't feel bad to admit that you don't know what to do. Not knowing is the beginning of being able to think and talk about the situation, and to begin to understand what the problem actually is.

→ Realise that 'having a problem' is not 'bad' or 'wrong'. Problems help us to think and understand more in order to move forward

If what you are doing is not working, - do something different. Anything.

Electronic Screens and Arrested Development
Be careful with modern electronic devices such as TV, educational DVDs, videos, computer games, iPhone applications as they reduce a child's time of direct human social interactions with other people, which can lead to very serious communication, relationship and development problems. The child's mind is instead filled up with persistent images that block the development of his own imagination. Sitting still is exactly the opposite if what toddlers need, which is to actively explore space and distance of their own body as much as possible.

WARNING!

Observe and think about

what are the underlying reasons/ triggers for the inappropriate behaviour:

Behaviour: What happens? (describe what actually happens, not what you think happens)

Time: When does it happen?

People: Who is present? Who does it happen with or to? How do others respond?

Feelings: How is the child/other people feeling? What is the emotional atmosphere?

Place: Where does it happen?

Situation: What is/was going on at the time and just before? Who or what triggers it?

Manner: How does s/he do it? What feelings can you identify in the child and in yourself?

Possible reasons:

→ changes in child's daily routine/ habitual activities,

→ confusion or fear because of unexpected changes,

→ child cannot understand what adults say (explanations, instructions, reassurance),

→ child cannot communicate what he wants/needs/feels,

→ child does not like being forced to do something that is too difficult, goes on for too long, is boring, ...

Family-Rules

Children need clear family rules to help them to make sense of the world and to build healthy minds. Because every family is different, family-rules will be different in every family. But they will always include events and daily routines that happen every day, e.g. brushing teeth, having a wash after getting up and before going to bed, sitting down when eating, eating healthily (and not eating sweets all the time), asking and using words rather than whinging and demanding, holding hands when crossing the road, etc. All young children need a bedtime routine to help them to go to sleep safely so they are rested and ready to play the next day. Children need guidance to learn how to listen and pay attention, to sit down to eat, to concentrate and play, to use the toilet and to behave in socially acceptable ways.

Boundaries and consequences:

Children also need clear boundaries so they know what happens in their family, if they don't listen and don't behave well, i.e. what the consequences are, including 'time-out', a 'thinking chair'. It is often a good idea to have a 'family meeting' to discuss new rules that have become necessary.

This boy was so angry. Without help he could not stop himself behaving like a monster

This boy has horrible feelings raging inside his mind. What is he going to do? His parents are frightened too

The horrible feelings become like a monster. But his parents are running away!

This mother is helping her child to calm down

Rules For Confident Parenting

1. Basic Rules:
1. **You, the parent/ adult, must be in charge** (not the child).
2. **Every child has a right to feel their feelings** and needs help to learn to manage these feelings appropriately, rather than acting them out by screaming or being indulged.
3. **It is not the parent's job to make the child happy.** It's the parent's job to think about how to enable the child to make him/herself happy and to support the child's efforts in this.

2. Be Pro-active! Make sure that
1. child does as much her/himself as s/he possibly can, i.e. **Don't do for her/him what s/he can do her/himself**, e.g. dressing, eating, tidying up, hanging up coat
2. **you spend time every day playing with your child** (at least 30 minutes), e.g. turn taking, action songs, looking at books together
3. child has **daily physical exercise and fresh air** to feed his brain and burn off energy, e.g. playground, swimming, running/ skipping around block of flats, small trampoline + provide warm clothes when cold, wellies/ raincoat when raining, so he can go out safely

3. Positive Communication
1. **Stay calm, be patient and don't shout** (i.e. speak slowly, give clear instructions).
2. **Tell him what to do, not what not to do:** make sure child knows what is expected of him/her and in which order to do it: 'First this, then that'.
3. **Reward good behaviour**, e.g. praise, a warm and appreciative look or hug, a reward.

4. Safe and Clear Boundaries:
1. **Hurting someone (self or other) or damaging the environment is never ok,** as it makes the child feel unsafe, frightened and insecure.
2. Aim for **Prevention** whenever possible: **Don't wait for child 'not to do it', or expect him to change his behaviour first**, – but remove things that he may throw/ bite/ pull/ ...
3. It is the **Adult's Responsibility** to **protect** the child, themselves, others and the environment from being hurt or damaged. It can be helpful to say calmly: 'I can see that you are angry/upset. But I cannot let you hurt people or damage things. I will help you manage your feelings (e.g. I will hold your hands, feet, head, put the toys away, ...) until you calm down.')

5. Responding to Tantrums/ Inappropriate/ Challenging behaviours:
1. **Be Boring**: avoid exciting responses, ignore it, i.e. **don't shout** when he has thrown something, but silently and boringly give him something else to do
2. **Be Consistent** (behaviour gets worse if you sometimes shout, sometimes ignore, sometimes give something nice to eat)
3. **Never undermine another adult** who is dealing with the child and a difficult behaviour (discuss different views afterwards and not in front of the child)

6. Create a Supportive Environment:
1. **Storage and Structure**: provide storage boxes, drawers, shelves,... so child knows where things are and where to tidy them up
2. encourage **Purposeful Activity** + ensure s/he is not bored + knows what to do next, i.e. give him things to do, involve him in everyday tasks (e.g. put away shopping, cooking),
3. provide sufficient **Toys and Play Activities** for all areas of development: fine-motor, perception, language, memory, imaginative play, singing, cognitive, gross-motor
4. **Avoid machines/ battery-operated/ electrical/ other 'Lazy' Toys**, i.e. limit TV, videos, computer to no more than 1 hour a day (e.g. use a wall chart, clock, egg timer)

In the Family: A Picture Book for Parents
'Effective Parenting and Behaviour Management'
By Sibylle Janert, 2004
To buy the PictureBook @ £10 +p/p www.mindbuilders-consulting.org

This picture-book looks at how to manage a number of everyday situations with your child. They are small examples of simple ideas for you to practice, on behaviour and parenting issues to show what it is like to be a parent and how little children learn to be social. It illustrates 15 simple key messages, with flaps to open, with the idea to prompt the reader to think about, and actively make sense of the 'stories', thus laying the foundation for reflective parenting.

What every parent needs to know
How parenting, behaviour and brain development are linked together
By Margot Sunderland, Dorling Kindersley (2007), ISBN-10: 1405320362

'A practical guide on sleep, crying, play and building emotional wellbeing for life. ... Based on over 700 scientific studies into children's development, BMA award-winning author and child psychotherapist Dr. Margot Sunderland explains how to develop your child's potential to the full. Find out the truth about popular childcare tactics, how touch, laughter and play build emotional wellbeing for life, and the strategies for effectively dealing with temper tantrums and tears. This is the first practical parenting book to give you the facts, not the fiction on the best way to bring up your child, essential for any parent.'

Touchpoints: The Essential Reference – Your Child's Emotional and Behavioral Development
By Dr. Berry Brazelton, Da Capo Lifelong Books (1992), ISBN-10: 020162690X

'Based on Dr. T. Berry Brazelton's extensive clinical practice and research, the Touchpoints approach emphasizes the building of supportive alliances between parents and providers around key points in the development of young children. 'Touchpoints' are predictable periods in a child's development that can disrupt family relations. These are times of disorganization that we value as opportunities to support family strengths and optimize children's development' www.touchpoints.com

Children in the Family:
Growing up and being Brought up

How do children grow up?

Children don't just grow up and development does not just happen automatically. Healthy development is a result of rich and varied interactions between the child and his environment, both with people and with the things around him. Although each child is born with certain traits, temperament, strengths and weaknesses, it is the relationship and interactions with their environment, and especially with their parents, that determine each child's progress and development, i.e. to what extent his parents support and encourage their child to develop his strengths and weaknesses.

'Touchpoints'
and Developmental Progress

The mind builds itself in interaction with other human beings. The interactive nature of human development means that development is never linear, but a process of continuous moments of crisis of 'catastrophic change': when a new idea comes into the mind, it creates chaos and turbulence by disrupting the current status quo in the personality, thus forcing previous ideas to be revised. New and unfamiliar ways have to be found because the 'old ways' are no longer suitable and need to be given up, – and we all know that change is difficult. These moments of crises that precede new developmental gains are what Dr. Brazelton calls 'Touchpoints': painful periods of change and transition from one state of mind to another that require the child and his family to adapt to. But these experiences of 'catastrophic change' are essential and unavoidable for a child's healthy mental development and progress.

Developmental achievements build on each other in a process of continuous crises of 'catastrophic change', – leading at each turning point either to 'breakdown' or 'break-through'.

This baby is calling out loudly, – not yet in words, but her meaning is clear: 'Mummy, where are you! I can't see you!' Having lost her mum is a problem, if you are just 1 year old

But this baby knows how to think and problem-solve. She has a plan: perhaps mum is upstairs? And off she goes to deal with her problem and to find out for herself

The one-year-old looks with wonder at the new baby, – the dummy in her hand shows that she is still pre-occupied with issues around weaning herself. The older boy's smile tells us that he understands that this new baby is special to his mum

The Major Turning Points of a Child's Development

Based on discussions with Franco Scabbiolo

1. Coming into being: PRE-BIRTH
The first experience of being and coming to know the sensations and sounds while in utero.

2. The shock of coming into the world: BIRTH
Being pushed out of the warm safe 'inside' of his mother's womb at birth means that the baby has to adapt to a totally new world of experiences full of sensations, sounds, sights, feelings and relationships.

3. The pleasure of being a baby: Feeling in control of the BREAST/BOTTLE
The discovery of 'finding a match' that meets his needs exactly, when his hungry mouth finds the nipple and tastes its milk for the first time fills the baby with wonder and love for more.

4. Mourning the loss of being a baby: WEANING
Having to come to terms with the sadness over the loss of the breast/bottle 'changes the mind' and opens new opportunities for the emergence of imagination of growing up and looking forward to moving out into the big wide world.

5. Wanting to be big like mum/dad: RIVALS
Becoming more aware of the world around him, the child begins to feel jealous of other people, of his siblings, but particularly of his parent(s) and he wants to be like them.

6. Realising that growing up takes effort: Having to abandon being SELF-CENTRED
It comes as a shock when the baby realises that his babbling isn't actually talking yet, and that he has to make an effort to learn, to listen, to pay attention and to practice.

7. Learning to control himself: TOILET TRAINING
For the first time in his life it is the mother/carer who asks the baby to give something to her that belongs to him (= his wee and pooh), and he has to accept 'how we do things here' (= use the toilet), because there are good things and bad things, – and the 'bad things' must be thrown away.

8. Becoming one of many: STARTING SCHOOL/NURSERY
Becoming part of a group means giving up the status of being 'mummy's special baby' and becoming 'one of the big children'. It requires being able to deal with loss by keeping mum in mind in his imagination and to stand his ground in the emotional turmoil of his peers.

9. Wanting to fit in with peers: ADOLESCENCE
The peer group now becomes the most important influence and the child becomes a stranger to his family, competing with parents about being grown up.

Making Time to Play at Home

The mind building nature of daily routines

Routines and daily rhythms help a child to make sense of their world and to build their mind ready for talking and all other learning. Routines are activities that happen regularly and have a clear predictable structure, which makes them ideal for encouraging turn-taking and interaction, e.g. mealtime and bedtime routines, the 'going out into the garden routine' (socks, shoes, coat, open the door ...), the 'wind the bobbin up' routine, the 'going in the car with mummy' vs. 'going in the car with daddy' routines ...

'Let's check whose turn it is.' Rotas and calendars can be very helpful, even before a child can read, because they help to 'lay down the law' and share organisation

A routine has

1. *a clear BEGINNING – MIDDLE – END, i.e. specific steps that*
2. *always happen in the same order, so you can look forward to the next bit, and*
3. *repeated regularly and many times, so you remember what's coming*
4. *with clear roles for each person, ideal to encourage turn-taking.*

Food and Eating

In order to be able to play and learn, children need to eat a healthy diet. But it is not just about getting food into a child, like putting petrol into a car. The food we eat feeds our mind and soul as well as our body. In order to eat, a child must be relaxed and wanting to eat. He needs to have an appetite. Seeing and smelling the food stimulates the digestive processes. It gets the mouth to produce saliva and the stomach to produce the digestive juices, so that we can swallow and digest our food well. Tense and nervous children cannot eat or digest their food properly. In fact, the stomach only produces the necessary digestive juices, if the person is relaxed and enjoys his food. If the atmosphere is tense or he feels stressed or pressurised, his body cannot digest the food.

Children need a relaxed atmosphere in order to eat and enjoy their food

A light-hearted playful approach to food and eating is therefore the most promising to encourage happy eating behaviours and a healthy balanced diet.

Allowing children to explore their food with hands and mouth helps them to understand the world

Good Healthy Food: 5 Food Groups

1. Vegetables and Fruit
2. Starchy foods/ carbohydrates: bread, potatoes, rice, pasta, chapattis, cereals, grains
3. Fats: oil, butter, margarine, ghee
4. Vitamins, Minerals, Spices
5. Protein:
   a. Vegetable Protein: beans, pulses, soya, nuts, seeds
   b. Animal Protein: meat, fish, chicken,
   c. Diary and Eggs: milk, yoghurt, cheese, diary products

A choice of healthy foods with different textures to explore

Non-foods: although these may taste nice, these are NOT nutritional, and therefore not really 'food'. Sugar rots children's teeth and chemical additives affect children's brain and behaviour:

→ Sugar: sweets, chocolate, biscuits, cake
→ Soft Drinks: sugary and fizzy drinks (except real fruit juice, – although even too much juice is bad for teeth!)
→ Additives, E-numbers, colourings, preservatives, sweeteners, chemicals

Bad foods: these foods are full of chemicals and have a low nutritional value:

→ White bread
→ Processed/ ready-cooked meals /fast food
→ Sugary foods and drinks, sweets, cake
→ Salty foods

WARNING!

Many young children suffer terrible toothache from being given sweets every day. Often the only 'solution' is an operation with full anaesthetic to have their rotting baby teeth taken out.

How much food is good for my child?

Children are born knowing when they are hungry and when they are full. Nobody needs to teach them. Babies cry to tell us that they are hungry, and stop eating when they are full. It is very important to trust a child's internal 'hunger-clock' that tells them to eat as much or as little as their bodies need, some days more and other days very little. It usually balances out over the course of a week or so. Children have different calorie needs. Some children don't need very much, and many children need less food than their worried parents believe.

Minimal Daily Diet for Under 4s

© Sibylle Janert, MA
☎ 07726 726 729

Does your child
EAT
something like this
most days?

Then you don't need to worry, says Child Development Expert
Dr. Berry Brazelton in his book 'Touchpoints' to Parents, e.g.:

- **1 pint/4 oz.** of DAIRY product: milk/yoghurt/cheese/dairy ice-cream
  = some cereal with milk + 1 yoghurt + cheese (matchbox-size) or similar per day
- **2 oz./100g** PROTEIN: fish, meat, egg, beans/lentils + **an iron supplement**
  = 1 egg and 2-3 bites of fish/(baked) beans/dhal/meat or similar per day
- **1 ounce/50g** fresh FRUIT or fruit juice (no added sugar):
  = $\frac{1}{2}$ glass orange-juice or $\frac{1}{2}$ apple/orange/peach, some grapes or similar per day
- **1 small piece** of VEGETABLE or 1 multi-vitamin tablet
  = a few peas, some carrot/tomato/cucumber/broccoli/potato or similar per day
- **Half a slice of whole-grain BREAD/CEREAL + some FAT/BUTTER/OIL**

www.mindbuilders-consulting.org

Less is more: Keep portions small

→ A child's stomach is about the size of his fist.

→ So it is best to keep portions small.

→ This allows the child the satisfaction of having finished all the food on his plate, and the power to ask for more.

→ Or give him a bowl with a picture at the bottom, which shines through when he has eaten all the food.

→ Giving a child too much food is not a kind thing to do, because it pushes the child into a negative position of rejecting food (because his stomach is full and he cannot eat it), thus setting up potential eating difficulties.

→ In fact, giving him 'not enough' is the kindest as it allows the child to finish what's on his plate, to feel proud for having done 'a good job' and to ask for more, thus encouraging social interaction and language development.

Keep portions small. He can always ask for more, which helps his language development

Eating the Food: Whose Job is it?

It is very important to remember that adults and children have different roles and responsibilities in order to avoid power battles around food and eating:

The Parent's Job is:

→ to provide a balanced diet with a variety of healthy and nutritious food at mealtimes and for snacks

→ to decide the What?, the Where? and the When? of eating, i.e. the adult decides what food is on offer today, that the child sits down at the table to eat and at regular times

→ to create a relaxed family atmosphere for orderly enjoyable mealtimes together

A parent's job is to decide on the What?, Where? and When? of eating

The Child's Job is:

→ to select what goes into his mouth

→ to choose what he will eat of the food the parent serves that mealtime

→ to put the food into his own mouth, using his own hands, spoon, fork etc., i.e. to feed himself

→ to decide how much to eat, or even whether to eat at all

A child's job is to decide what goes into his mouth and how much to eat

How to encourage Healthy Eating

Children need a variety of foods so they get all the nutrients (such as protein, carbohydrate, fat, vitamins, and minerals, – except sugar, which is not a food) they need for normal growth over the course of a week or so.

→ **Buy the right food** (i.e. food that is wholesome and healthy), prepare it nutritiously (e.g. boiling and baking is healthier than frying) and serve it creatively. If you don't buy sweets or fizzy drinks or keep them in the house, then your child won't be able to eat them, and his teeth won't rot. Easy.

→ **Provide a suitable place** for the child to sit, e.g. high enough so he can easily reach his plate on the table (add cushions so his upper arms can hang down) and support his feet so they don't dangle, which is distracting (and likely to lead to mischief).

→ **Set a reliable mealtime routine with clear boundaries:**
  • a regular place, a friendly atmosphere, sitting at a table
  • regular times: breakfast, snack, lunch, snack, dinner
  • after-school snack to be an interesting and healthy finger-food time (not crisps every day!)
  • food only when sitting down, and not inbetween mealtimes

→ **Sit down to eat**. Food and drink stay on the table when the child gets up. This also keeps mess in one place and helps children to be mindful for whoever has to clean up food that gets dragged all around the house.

→ **Create a calm relaxed environment** where the focus is on enjoying eating food together, including talking about the food, where it comes from, who cooked or bought it, who likes what, how much is left, ...

→ **Stick to 3 meals a day (breakfast, lunch, dinner) and 2 snacks** inbetween, so the child has time to play and use his mind (rather than his mouth) for playing and thinking about things other than food, to learn to wait, to feel hungry/thirsty, and full again after the meal

→ **Eat together as a family** every day and as often as possible. Keep family meals pleasant and positive.

→ **Expect erratic eating in a young child**. Aim for a nutritiously balanced week, not a balanced day.

→ **New foods:** Research shows that children need to be offered new foods more than 15 times before they will try and like them. So don't be discouraged by his disinterest or rejection. Just continue to provide a small amount of new foods. Eventually he will become interested and taste it. Perhaps he may like it, or not.

→ **Include your child in food preparations**, including cooking, setting the table for everyone and clearing up.

→ **Make physical activity a part of your family's daily life**. Go to the park or playground every day. Take a walk after dinner. Consider 'charging' your child 15 minutes of active play (running, bike, tag, ball games, ...) for every 15 minutes of TV or computer time. This will build up your child's appetite for healthy foods and help with digestion.

REMEMBER:
Providing a balanced diet and a relaxed family atmosphere is the parent's job.

What NOT to do:

→ **Do NOT eat in front of the TV** and switch off all electronic screens, so your child can engage with his food and talk with you about his food or other things he has in mind. (If a young child will only eat with the TV on, this may indicate or become a serious problem with relationships, and you should seek help and advice.)

→ **Do NOT provide sweets, snacks and drinks (except water) inbetween mealtimes** as it damages your child's appetite and teeth. These are not actually food, are full of chemicals and have no nutritional value.

→ **Do NOT make comments about how much or what food your child eats.** Pressure to eat actually reduces a child's acceptance of new or different foods.

→ **Do NOT sit over your child watching every spoonful he puts into his mouth. Have something to eat yourself,** so you are eating together and your child can see you eating healthy food.

→ **Do NOT take it personally,** if your child doesn't like one or the other food that you have cooked or provided. Being picky is part of a young child's 'job'. He is just practicing his own personal choices. But he still loves you. **Take the credit, but don't take the blame.**

REMEMBER:
Eating and deciding what goes into their mouth/body is the child's and NOT a parent's job.

FOOD IS FUN and learning about food is fun, too. Eating foods from the Food Guide Pyramid and being physically active will help you grow healthy and strong.

The Food Pyramid shows the 5 different food groups and gives an idea of which foods to eat more of, especially vegetables and fruit. We need to help children to eat less sweets, crisps and snacks full of fat, salt and sugar

Being playful with food and helping in the kitchen

Children love to play and to discover imaginative ways of dealing with everyday activities. Children need to be allowed to explore their food in order to find out about how the world works, what things feel, taste, smell and look like.

Children love to be involved and to help in the kitchen. Cooking and especially baking with your child also encourages language development and thinking, remembering what comes next, then waiting for it to be ready and to share the food together:

→ *baking cake, biscuits, pizza*

→ *peeling cucumber, carrots, potatoes with a potato-peeler*

→ *washing potatoes, vegetables, lentils*

→ *shelling fresh peas, broad beans*

→ *preparing vegetables, e.g. using an onion cutter, or supervised by a responsible adult with a sharp knife*

→ *grating cheese*

→ *making mashed potato*

→ *setting the table for everyone in the family*

→ *washing up*

→ *sorting cutlery into the drawer and putting away clean dishes*

→ *mopping the floor*

Being playful around food and eating helps everyone in the family to feel relaxed with each other

He's washed them, and now he is watching the potatoes change colour as granddad peels them

Some simple recipes

Pizza:
Ingredients:
Packet of pizza base
Tomato paste
Grated cheese
Mushrooms, tomatoes, ham, salami, courgette, … other vegetables
Put mix into large bowl
Mix with water
Knead on floured board
Roll or pat into shape
Topping:
Spread tomato paste onto the base with the back of teaspoon
Cut up vegetable
Grate the cheese
Add vegetables, ham, … and grated cheese
Leave to rise
Cook in the oven
Sit down and eat together

Making Pizza

Fish cakes:

Ingredients: Mashed potato, Tin of tuna,
1 Egg, Bread crumbs
Mix mashed potato and tuna
Mix and make into patties
Whisk the egg
Dip patties into egg,
Roll in bread crumbs
Cook with a little oil in frying pan or
oven until hot and golden brown
Eat and enjoy!

Banana or strawberry yoghurt:

Ingredients: Plain yoghurt, banana, ripe
and/or strawberries, mango, peaches,
apricots ...
Squash banana/strawberries with a fork
Mix with yoghurt
Eat and enjoy!

Some simple creative eating-ideas that are easy to do, but will delight your child:

→ broccoli trees in a mashed potato field with cauliflower sheep
→ sandwich face with carrot eyes and tomato mouth on a sandwich
→ cucumber 'teeth': biting into a thick slice of cucumber
→ a baked potato car with carrot wheels and a spoon as the driver
→ an orange sun with kiwi clouds and raisins for rain and an apple crescent as moon
→ rain from chickpeas or rice or grapes
→ snow from rice, mashed potato
→ a mountain from mashed potato, rice or pasta with a broccoli tree on top
→ a dog/cat made from 4 sticks of carrot with half-an-apple as body and a grape as head

Cauliflower-sheep and a broccoli-tree: using the imagination and making stories helps many children to want to engage with and eat their food

Helping mum in the kitchen with the red peppers before the age of 1

Children love it, when their food smiles at them

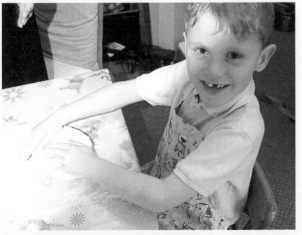

Making dough for bread or pizza is a great sensory activity. And later you can eat and share it too

Baking together is a wonderful activity to share, with basic ingredients like flour transformed into lovely cakes

Taking the rubbish out is part of learning about good and bad, right and wrong, clean and dirty

With adult supervision, already small children can help prepare vegetables and help in the kitchen. And they love it

Eating problems

In order to avoid eating problems, it is important to allow the child to eat by himself, so he is free to figure out and decide what he wants to eat, as well as exploring the textures, consistency, colours of his food, what happens when you mix them, etc.

Eating problems are very stressful for parents. Avoid power struggles, – and find someone to support you!

Strategies for dealing with Eating Problems:
If you have ended up with eating problems, here are some basic ideas and strategies:

→ **Develop trust and emotional engagement with the child** *overall and don't just focus on eating, e.g. by enjoying playing together at times other than eating times*

→ **NEVER force-feed a child**, *i.e. always respect a child saying 'No, I don't want to take this into my mouth'*

→ *The child is not necessarily motivated by hunger, i.e. being hungry may not make him ask or look for food and not asking for food/drink does not necessarily mean that he isn't hungry/thirsty*

→ *Don't go too fast:* **take your time***, don't rush and give the child enough space and time*

→ **Relax** *and make sure, that you don't put your own anxieties into the child*

→ **Avoid power struggles** *at all costs*

→ *Don't give too much. In fact giving 'not enough' encourages your child to ask for more and to give him the satisfaction of 'eating it all' and finishing what's on his plate.*

→ *Get the child to engage with new food in any way he can, e.g. touch it, sniff it, spit it out, ...*

→ **NEVER trick or force the child**

→ *If child has very limited choice of foods he eats, then respect this and don't mess with these foods.*

Bedtimes Routines:
Sleep gets us ready to play

Children need to be 'parented' to go to sleep, not just put to sleep. Learning to let oneself drop off to sleep takes time and most children need help to learn this. It requires us to feel relaxed to let go of our conscious thinking and to allow ourselves to drift off and into our dream-world. Children who get used to always sleeping with their parent will find it harder to go to sleep by themselves or to cope when they wake up at night, because they become used to using someone's body rather than their own mind to manage their feelings. This makes night time and sleeping problems more likely for the whole family. It is helpful to encourage a child to bring their favourite teddy to bed with them every night to cuddle, and so they don't need to feel so alone.

Children need to be 'parented' to go to sleep. They need help to learn to let themselves drop off to sleep

Night time parenting is mostly the art of calming things down and creating a soothing atmosphere that allows the child to relax and get ready for sleep, and to have some quality time with their parent(s). For children, bed time is reassurance time. By developing a predictable bedtime routine for you and your child, you encourage healthy sleeping habits for your child and avoid many of the problems that may arise when it is time to turn out the lights. Consistent bedtime routines and rituals set the child up to expect that sleep is to follow and help everyone to make the transition from day to night, from waking to sleeping and dreaming.

Children's brains are a work in progress until they are 21. Much of what the day's learning happens at night while asleep

How much sleep do children need?

Children need enough sleep for the brain to grow and a lot of learning in fact happens while asleep! Research shows that children who sleep more are better at school and learn and remember more. Sleep before midnight is the most important for brain growth. It is therefore very important that children go to bed early enough to get as many hours of sleep as possible before midnight, i.e. bedtime for children under 5 should be 7pm, if they get up at 7am.

If a 4-year-old child needs about 12 hours of sleep per night, she needs to go to bed by 7pm in order to be up by 7am

0-3 months old	18 hours/night
Babies up to 3 years	14 hours/night
Children between 3-5 years	12 hours/night
Children between 5-10 years	10-12 hours/night
Adolescents	8-10 hours/night
Adults	8 hours/night

Planning a bedtime routine

Establishing a bed time routine is not going to happen overnight. You will need a plan and then stick with it. Start by thinking about your family's time-table, your child's age and needs, the number of hours of sleep a child his age needs, what time you need to get up to get ready for school without having to rush. Decide what time suits your family, and stick with that time. Get a night-light, if your child is frightened of the dark.

Review of the Day at Bedtime: a few minutes to process with dad what happened today prepare the child for tomorrow, so he does not have to take unresolved issues into the night and his dreams

Bed time is a time to slow down

Take time to slow down the pace and allow the child to wind down. Don't ask your child to stop suddenly what he is doing or playing. Children need to be given plenty of warning that it is almost time to get ready for bed. Help him to clear up, – and keep a happy smile in a friendly atmosphere. Bedtime should be a quiet, pleasant and relaxed time.

Settling teddy or doll into bed, helps the child to think about going to bed and play out the bedtime routine symbolically with his toys

Bedtime routine for a young child

Until 5.15 pm   *Play*

5.15 pm *Tidy up, switch off TV/ computer, set the table, get ready for dinner*

5.30 pm *Have dinner together*

6pm   *Involve children in clearing up kitchen and washing up*

6.15 pm *Get ready for bath time*

6.30 pm *Bath time (see next section on Bath Time)*

7.00 pm *Get into bed, arrange the covers and get the child's favorite teddy settled in bed too.*

7.05 pm *Bedtime story and singing a lullaby, starting with simple picture books and progressing to chapter books, reading a chapter every night.*

7.15 pm *Review of the day: How are you feeling? What's on your mind? How was today? What is going to happen tomorrow? Talking about dreams*

7.25 pm *Bed time songs, prayers, hugs, kisses and tucking the covers in. Plug in night-light.*

7.30 pm *Lights out! Perhaps play a soothing music CD.*

Healthy bedtimes

→ Encourage your child to settle their favorite teddy or doll into bed before they go to bed themselves. This helps the child to think about going to bed and play out the bedtime routine symbolically with their toys.

→ Children should have NO television for about 1-2 hours before bed. Television, video games and digital devices have an unsettling effect on the mind, interfere with brain activity needed for dream-thoughts and do not lend themselves to restfulness like a lullaby or bedtime story does.

Brushing teeth is part of these toddlers' bedtime routine

→ Respect the natural order of things, i.e. that younger children need more sleep and should go to bed earlier, thus starting their bed time routine earlier than their older siblings. Children should also be in bed before their parents' bedtime.

→ Parents need to have some grown-up time to themselves to keep their sanity, to recover from the day, talk to each other and prepare for tomorrow.

Even dolly needs to have her teeth brushed before going to bed

WARNING!

TV in bedroom
→ Deprives a child of a month's sleep a year
→ Even passive viewing in a room contributes to sleep difficulties in 5-6 year olds

Review of the day at bedtime

Even with a baby, you can sit on the child's bed and let the events of the day pass through your mind and describe the sequence of events, perhaps remembering again what happened in the morning, where you went, what the child did alone and what you did together. With an older child, the parent wants to do more listening and less talking. And remember: this is not a time for teaching, but for sharing and talking and listening. Go through the 3 key-questions and be open to talk about dreams, listen to your child and take some time to enjoy seeing out a day together and preparing for a new tomorrow:

1. **How are you feeling?** *What's on your mind?*
2. **How was today?** *What did you like best today? What was not so good? What worried or upset you? How did it happen? Is there anything you learn from this, even though it felt 'bad'? What could you try next time in order for it to be better?*
3. **What is going to happen tomorrow?** *What are you looking forward to? What are you worried about? Is there anything you really want to do/achieve/avoid tomorrow?*
4. **Talking about dreams.** *Everybody dreams when asleep and although we often don't remember our dreams, they can have a powerful impact on a child. Sometimes they seem to solve problems. At other times they turn into nightmares, that can wake us up. Then the child needs help to talk and think about his fears with his parents. Day-dreams are also important in sustaining our hope and plans for the future. What would be your best dream come true?*

Bedtime trouble and sleeping problems

If your child keeps coming out or won't stay in bed

→ **Return him to bed right away**.

→ **Tell him calmly and firmly** that 'It's bedtime. It's time to go to sleep.'

→ Show him with your **body language** that this is bedtime and NOT play-time: keep your voice low, your movements decisive, your touch business-like, don't switch on the light: the day is finished. The End.

→ **Be boring:** don't shout, don't explain, don't enter into conversation, do NOT engage in discussions or negotiations, do not provide food ... apart from repeating 'It's bedtime. It's time to go to sleep. ... If you are quiet and stay in bed, I will come to check on you in a few minutes.', by which time the child will usually be sound asleep.

Martin Waddell illustrated by Barbara Firth

Bedtime troubles are common. They respond to consistent clear messages that 'It's time to sleep now.'

→ If he keeps coming out of bed, **keep returning him to bed**, – again and again (perhaps 20 times), following the same 'boring' routine as above, until your child realises that there is no point, that you are going to be 'boring' and won't rise to his provocations, so he gives up on getting out of bed and goes to sleep.

→ Trust and believe that **yes, he CAN do it!** And, no, you are NOT a cruel parent. You are thinking ahead and helping your child to get enough sleep, so his brain can grow and he can be ready for a new day, feeling rested so he can play and do and learn lots of new things.

Playtime in the Bath

Bath time is a perfect way of helping a child to make the transition from the busy reality world of the day to the peaceful calm dream world of the night. Almost all children love having a bath, which can easily take up to 45 minutes, if hot water is added when necessary. That's up to 45 minutes of your child playing happily and learning about science every day! Sitting in the bath is a safe and soothing place to play and wind down, and the warm water gets children relaxed and ready for sleep. Children also sleep better, when they are clean. In fact it is a good idea to make bath time part of a child's daily bedtime routine, something you and your child can look forward to. It does not take much effort from the adult to make bath time into a magic time for both of you. The main ingredients are a little bit of planning, time and a few bath-time things.

Start by prioritising bath time, collect a few of the ingredients, and look forward to more relaxing evenings from now on. A whole bath time routine can easily take 1 hour, so if you want your child in bed by 7.30pm, you need to get started by 6pm or 6.30pm at the latest.

Young children find water fascinating: it flows, is gone, but keeps going. You can touch it, but not hold it, ...

Share and learn from each other

1. Decide what time suits your family as part of your whole bed time routine, and stick with that time.
2. Tidy up with your child before he gets ready for the bath.
3. Talk about what toys he would like to play with in the bath today.
4. Make sure you start early enough and leave enough time, so you don't need to rush or nag your child.
5. Get your child to help to run the water, get the toys and his pyjamas, get undressed, put dirty clothes into laundry basket, ...
6. Prepare his towel on the radiator nearby.
7. Let your child soak and play in the bath. Check the temperature occasionally.
8. Sit by the bath and join your child in his play.
9. He may like to play by himself for a bit, – or siblings with each other.
10. Teach him to keep the water inside the bath. If he keeps pouring it out or splashing too much, this ends today's bath-time. Simply lift him out and dry him. Be boring. Don't shout. Being boring is more effective in getting the child to think about what went wrong. Shouting can easily become a game or a power battle. But tomorrow, do bath-time again, – same routine as above. That way he will learn best.
11. Give your child several warnings before it is time to come out of the bath, so he can prepare himself, i.e. 'Soon it will be time to come out', 'In 5 minutes it will be time ...', 'I'm coming to wash you and then it'll be time to come out.'.
12. When it is finally time, have his towel ready as he steps out

Water Play in the Bath

Fill bath with warm water to reach child's belly button when he sits down:

1. *fill up a big empty container/bucket with a smaller container (empty yoghurt pot), sing/count until it is full*
2. *use a sponge/ empty shampoo bottle/ turkey baster/ eye dropper to fill a bigger container/bucket: 'in and squeeze'*
3. *poke a small hole into an empty plastic bottle and show the child that water comes out and that he can stop the water with his thumb: add 'stop!' – 'go!'; or make 2-5 holes for 2-5 fingers; lots of holes for a 'shower'*
4. *hum, with your chin and closed mouth in the water*
5. *blow ping pong balls/ corks across the water*
6. *'Fishing game' (see above)*
7. *become a 'seal', 'crocodile' (see 'Animal Walks')*

of the bath, and give him a good rub, perhaps apply oil or lotion, before he puts on his pyjamas ready to jump into bed … for his bedtime story …

Bath Time Activities

1. **Bubble bath:** Have an assortment of different bubble baths and bath salts (different colours and scents) for the child to choose from.

2. **Wash and scrub games:** there's a lot of interesting things one can do with a sponge or flannel apart from using it to get washed, like letting the water drip down, watching it sink, stuffing it into a container, squeezing it out, … Some children will also like body-brushes and massage mittens to use or play with.

3. **Bath-time toys:** playing with kitchen utensils has much higher play value than bought bath toys like boats and ducks (what else can you play with a bath duck than ducking him or watching him float?), e.g. sieves, whisks, measuring cups, jugs, plastic funnel, plastic bottles (some with holes punched in them). A plastic colander can double as an excellent storage basket. There could also be a selection of boats, ducks and other floating animals. Prepare 2-3 different sets to choose from, kept in small laundry bags, – for child to choose from. You should also allow your child to choose of 2 sets as he combining boats, bottles and flannels, or similar, may generate new ideas and activities.

4. **Warm towels and pyjamas:** especially nice in the winter months, children love to get out of the bath into a warmed towel and pyjamas! Little touches make all the difference.

5. **Poetry night in the bath:** collect suitable poems in the library and on the internet to read out and say together, – keep in splash proof plastic folder, or get them laminated.

6. **Shaving foam sculptures:** squirt some shaving foam onto the side of bath or into your child's hands (warn him to keep it away from his eyes) and let his imagination take over!

7. **Music and story CDs** to listen or sing along to.

8. **Candle light for special occasions:** only suitable for well-supervised bath times, but kids really do love the atmosphere of a candle lit bath. Light candles only when the children are in the bath, placed out of reach and with nothing above the flame and extinguish before they climb out to be completely safe.

Half an hour in the bath, where they can explore and play, is time well spent for small children

Big brothers helping the baby feel safe in the water

A lot of learning goes on in the bath: about in-out, floating – sinking, quantities, containers, temperature

Toilet Training:
Using the Toilet is a Young Child's New Game

The 2-year old sees something interesting floating in the toilet, just like the stuff she pushes into her nappy, and she thinks to herself 'Magic! How did THAT get in there? ... Amazing, the things big people can do. And how convenient! And mum and seem to like this place, they go there every day. ... I want to be able to do that too. ... What can I do to get my pooh in there?' This is the true beginning of toilet training: the child beginning to wonder how his body works and how to control it in order to grow up.

Using the potty or toilet is an important step in every child's development. But with disposable nappies many children nowadays never even see their pooh, which is swiftly covered up and whipped into a scented bag by mum as if it was nothing to do with the child. How can he then feel owner-ship of what after all is HIS pooh? How will he realise that his pooh/wee are in fact HIS responsibility, not mum's? Nor do 'modern children' feel uncomfortable enough to want to be-come clean and to 'do something about it'. This means that on average it takes up to 3 years longer for children in disposable nappies to become toilet-trained! If you'd have had the con-venience of full room service all your life, would you suddenly wish to give it up and decide to do your own cleaning? Some children do, but many need careful help and encouragement to become toilet-trained.

Toilet training a child is not just a matter of physically sitting a child on the toilet. It does not start with a bum-on-seat exercise, though this plays a part. Toilet training starts with helping the child to understand about 'good' and 'bad', 'clean' and 'dirty', 'right' and 'wrong'. It's about realising that there are things that need to be thrown away, and that there is a 'right' place for the 'bad' stuff. If pooh goes on the walls or carpet, we find this disgusting. It's ok in the toilet, because this is the 'right' place for the 'bad' disgusting stuff. Babies in fact don't initially find things disgusting, not even their pooh or wee. This is the time for them to learn about what's ok and what's disgusting.

Finding a way to give up the nappy:

Sitting around the table with her family, the little girl happily informed everybody: 'I'm now going to make my nappy all nice and warm.' If nappies make the child feel too comfortable, it will be more difficult to give them up and to use a cold toilet seat instead. We need to help her to realise the advantages of the toilet instead the nappy.

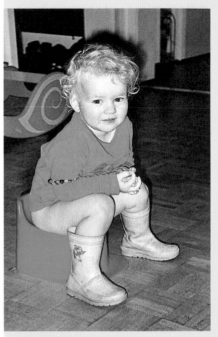

Most young children between 21 and 23 months find using the potty an interesting new activity

Becoming toilet trained is about differentiating between
- → *good and bad*
- → *right and wrong*
- → *precious and valuable*
- → *in and out*
- → *there and gone*
- → *here and there*
- → *this way, not that way*
- → *our way, not your way/ social not self(ish)*
- → *clean/tidy and dirty/messy/ unhygienic/disgusting*
- → *safe and dangerous*
- → *assertive and submissive*
- → *regulated and chaotic*
- → *development and stagnation*
- → *obedience and defiance*
- → *freedom and adaptation*
- → *communication and manipulation*
- → *cooperativeness and tyranny/ blackmailing*
- → *order and anarchy*

Toilet training has to be introduced by parents:
Together, parents and child need to find a way together to leave the nappy behind.
If toilet training is delayed too much, there will be all sorts of problems with school and growing up.

In order to be toilet-trained, a **child needs to be**
→ interested in the sensations and what happens at their bottom-end and in their wee and pooh
→ aware of when they 'need to go', i.e. when their wee/pooh is coming, – but most importantly
→ able to 'hold it', despite the urgency, in order to get to the toilet/potty in time, and
→ to want to do their mum/dad a favour, because this toilet-issue seems to be so important to grown-ups.

In order to start toilet-training and to prevent confusion **parents have to**
→ introduce the idea of rules and different places to the child: kitchen for food, bedroom for sleeping, bathroom for washing, toilet for pooh/wee (= first lessons in geography!)
→ give clear boundaries: 'This is how it's done.'
→ have clear expectations: 'I know that you can do this, and I expect you to do it this way.'
→ help child to regulate his physical processes, i.e. help him to notice, when he needs to go to do a wee or pooh
→ to find a way together with their child to leave the nappy behind
→ be consistent, reliable, regular, determined and clear
→ keep going, weather set-backs, fears and disappointments … and help the child to succeed.

This toy-dog is carefully helped to use the potty by his competent 2-year-old owner, who knows how to do 'it' and thinks it is a very good game

The beginnings of toilet training: the one-year-old sister looks on with interest at what her brother and his toy-dog can do. Toilet training starts like this inside a child's mind wondering 'How does he do it?'

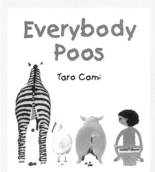

Everybody poos.
By Taro Gomi. Frances Lincoln Children's Books (2004), ISBN-10: 1845072588

Many children, and their parents, have found this simple picture book very helpful in thinking and talking about pooh and becoming confident with using the toilet.

TOILET TRAINING:
Learning to use the toilet is in fact a psychological issue that is to do with organising the mind. It's about knowing what goes where and that there are clear routines. Therefore, children with clear bedtime routines and predictable mealtimes are likely to find it easier to become toilet-trained than those from families where things happen whenever wherever.

How to start Toilet Training:

→ Start when you can devote a lot of time to helping your child to 'get it': you will need to show him, take him frequently to the toilet/potty, find new ways of showing him and explaining it, deal with accidents and set-backs, fears and disappointments, defiance and loss of confidence, your child's as well as yours.

→ Get a potty or a toilet-inset and a stool for the child to rest his feet on, so he can push against it when having a bowel movement. Make sure the inset seat fits well and doesn't wobble, which makes some children feel insecure and anxious.

→ Get him to try out sitting on potty or toilet just like a chair, first perhaps with clothes on, just for fun.

→ Train boys to pee sitting down, it'll make it easier for him to understand the whole process. Otherwise he will have to learn 2 different ways to face the toilet depending on wee or pooh. What is he going to do, when both come at the same time? Progressing to standing up once he's 'got it' will be easy.

→ Create a routine (see routines)

→ Start to change him only in the toilet and standing up, because he's a 'big boy now': that's what toilet training is all about. Help him to realise he is growing up and no longer a baby.

→ Let him see his pooh in the nappy and talk about it

→ Drop his pooh into the toilet for him to see the new place for his pooh and that 'that's where the pooh goes!'.

→ Show him about the right places for the right things, i.e. pooh and wee in the toilet, rubbish in the bin, bath in the bathroom, food in the kitchen.

→ Give him the job of putting his dirty nappy into the bin, the good place for 'bad' things that need to be thrown away.

→ Ask him to take more responsibility himself, e.g. to find the bin and throw away his own rubbish like wrappers, banana skins, apple cores, used juice cartons ... rather than giving it to you to throw it away.

→ Let him see mummy, daddy and other people pee and pooh in the toilet: now isn't that amazing!? We need the child to start wondering: 'Hey! Magic! How did they do this? There was nothing in there before. But now there is! I want to be able to do this too! Who can help me to figure out how I can do it for myself?'

Making Space to Play at Home

Children need a Child-centred Home Environment where one can play freely

Children need space to play at home and somewhere to sit and be, and they need to go outside every day. Children also need things to explore and play with. They need play-materials that they can reach easily and whenever they need to without having to ask someone for permission. Children also need attention and genuine interest from their parents in order to develop well.

STRUCTURE AT HOME MEANS STRUCTURE IN YOUR CHILD'S MIND.
Research confirms that children from well-organised homes with space to play, clear daily routines and freely accessible storage for their play materials are more successful at school and in later life.

Structure at home means structure in the mind. Too many toys are confusing and don't help a child to play well. Often less is more

Children need a Space to Play at Home and somewhere to be

Children who grow up in small town-flats need space to play and it is very important to organise things in order to maximize the limited space available.

Creating Space in Small Flats:

Having bunk-beds helps to create the space in a small bedroom for playing, which is essential for children's mental health, as well as giving each child some personal private space to store their toys, books and personal things. Children love small spaces, where they can make a den, a play 'house' or curl up on cushions to read books or play.

In small inner city flats, bunk-beds are ideal as they create space for storage, and for playing or studying underneath

Somewhere to sit and play

Having a suitable place to sit and play makes all the difference in helping children to pay attention, concentrate and occupy themselves meaningfully. When children sit on an adult chair without a cushion or booster seat, the table comes to their shoulders and they are too low to be able to reach or use their arms. Try kneeling on the floor to eat your dinner or write a letter on the table: it's really uncomfortable and you won't want to do it for long. This is what it feels like for children who don't have suitable chairs.

Having a suitable chair and table to sit, makes all the difference to children's play and learning at home

Small sturdy table and chairs. These are from Ikea

'Come and sit in me!': This children's rattan arm chair invites the child to sit and stay. From Ikea

Two beds in a small room: Where would the children have space to play without the bunk bed?

Children love to be high up. Suitable for children up to the age of 7 or 8, this high-chair allows the child to reach the dining table and will make mealtimes much easier. From Ikea

Tripp Trapp chairs can be adjusted for babies and up to the age of 11

A small table and child-sized chairs to sit to draw or do other activities can make all the difference. Make sure the chair is solid so an adult can sit on them too, and your child can't easily tip over backwards. All young children love to be high up and a suitable high chair can really help with meal-times and table-top activities. The child loves to be 'up', – and it will take him a bit longer to get back down. Some families invest in a solid wooden high chair that can be adjusted along with the growing child.

Choosing a suitable chair for your child

It is essential that the child's upper arms can hang down and his lower arms can lie horizontally on the table top, either using a high chair or a low chair and low table. Otherwise he cannot reach and use his arms properly, and without being able to reach and use his arms, he cannot play, explore and learn well.

Children need their own Storage Space to organise their Play Materials

Even though there may be limited floor space, there is always space along the walls that can be used by putting up shelves. Then boxes can be stacked in the shelves or on top of each other. These must be easily accessible to a child and not require him to have to ask an adult for everything. Otherwise children may end up in front of the TV or computer, losing time to play and think, and for their brains to grow and develop.

Access to play materials and storage space

Children need space to play and things to play with. It is important for a child to be able to access different materials in play so they can express themselves using their imagination, which helps children to build their minds. Don't limit children in the use of materials. A box can be a car, rocket, bed, a hidey-hole or a shop. You can play in, on, under or with it. A brick can be a phone. A cushion and a blanket can make a bed, or a boat ….

Containers are key

Everything needs a home to be happy, even toys, e.g. shelves, boxes, containers. It is best to have several smaller contain-ers, so your child can learn to sort into different categories, e.g. all the cars together, a box for all the animals, another for pens and paper.

Small seats and table at the right height invite the children to sit and focus on their activity

Children need their own storage space to organise their play materials and toys. Trofast from Ikea is sturdy and versatile

Everything needs a home to be happy, even toys and play-materials, e.g. shelves, boxes, containers

AVOID large 'toy-boxes' full of unspecified "stuff", where nobody can find anything.

One container per activity

Have a container for all the parts of an activity: a container for the bricks, another container for small animals, a container for paper and a smaller one for pens. Boxes from the see-through plastic variety are particularly useful, as you and your children can see what is inside before even moving the box. Having containers and boxes also helps to develop responsibility in young children. Get them to clear up when they have finished with an activity. It is easy for them to see on their own, if they have done a good job or not: either all the parts are in the box or they are not!

Use labels

Labeling has two uses for families: labels promote literacy as well as organization. Make labels for each box to say what is inside. Don't do it alone but involve the child in the process of labeling. That way, they get to use the words that are most meaningful to them, which is an important part in making this a system they will find helpful to use. For young children who cannot yet read, you may either draw or cut out pictures; this is a pre-reading skill because the child learns that there is a relationship between a symbol and its meaning.

Containers are key: one container per activity helps to organise the toys, as well as the mind

Small drawer units

Small drawer units are a great play object for any child as well as useful storage. The drawers come out and can be stacked as a tower or made into cars or a doll's bed or used to store precious 'bits' according to categories. You can paint them, sit on them, label the drawers, stack the drawers on top of each other or even several units. And at the end, everything can be put away neatly.

Small drawer-units are a great play-object for any child as well as useful storage

Children need Space and Time
with TV and all Electronics switched off

When the TV is on in the room, or any other electronic screen, some or all of a child's (and adult's) attention is hijacked by its constantly moving colours and sounds, leaving no internal space for his own imagination, ideas or thinking. This is so damaging to children's brain and mental development that the American Association of Paediatricians recommend NO TV at all in their first 2 years and no more than 1 hour a day until the age of 5!

The TV talks a lot, but it does not listen. Children cannot play when their imagination is tied up with electronic images and they don't learn to talk, when there is nobody listening and paying attention to what they have to say. When the TV is on all the time, people talk less in families and children may end up with language-delay or other problems. Children need to be able to play freely using their own imagination in order to develop language and to build their mind.

In fact, research now shows that the brain of young children who watched more than 1 hour of TV a day are wired quite differently than those who had more interactive experiences with parents and other adults before they were 2 years old. There is also research that shows that for every hour of watching educational videos promising to help with language development, the young child learns 5 words LESS than a child who plays with other people and does not watch videos!

TV-zombies: nobody is talking, interacting, moving, playing ... or thinking. That's why paediatricians advise 'no more than 1 hour a day for young children'!

TV and screen-electronics steal the child's mind and imagination, filling it instead with electronic visual 'junk' that is very difficult to get rid of

'THE VAMPIRE OF THE MIND':
TV and screen-electronics suck out and steal the child's own pictures and imagination, filling it instead with electronic visual 'junk' that is unhealthy and very difficult to get rid of.

'Lazy toys' steal your child's mind and don't help him to play and learn

'Lazy toys' don't help your child to play

Watching electronic screens, whether TV, videos, mobiles, iPhones, computers or 'flashy flashy noisy noisy toys' inhibit children's imagination and language development. These are all 'lazy toys' that make a child's mind passive and 'lazy'. They don't help him to use his mind to think for himself. They fill up his mind with man-made visuals and steal his time from talking with others, exploring his ideas or playing imaginatively.

WARNING!

Children need Attention, Interest and Recognition

Children need attention and interactive regulation from their parents at home. Just buying toys and leaving children to get on with things by themselves when at home is not enough. If parents want their children to talk, learn and behave well, parents need to pay attention, listen and respond to them carefully. Children growing up in city flats need their parents to show genuine interest and spend time talking, listening and playing with their child at home every day. Children need recognition for who they are and for tasks well done.

Children need attention, interest and interactive regulation from their parents at home

Remember to turn off TV and other electronics. Where TV or computer are on all the time, people talk much less in families. So, if you want the best for your child, make sure, there is more time when TV, computer, mobiles etc. are OFF than when they are on! And do put your mobile phone away, when you are interacting with your child. And when you are with other people too. It's simply rude and disrespectful not to!

Every 'Negative' costs 7 'Positives'

Of course, children also need limits and boundaries. And sometimes children need to be told off. But research shows that children who get more negative than positive attention from their parents suffer mental-emotional damage resulting in behaviour and learning difficulties. According to Sue Jenner, the psychologist behind the 'Parent-Child Game' one 'negative' costs at least 7 positives, i.e. each time a child is told off, he will feel bad and need at least 7 positive 'attends' to recover and feel good about himself again.

FIVE A DAY OF PARENTING
(Chris Paterson: 'Parenting Matters')
1. Playing with your child on the floor
2. Talking to your child and listening without distractions (i.e. NOT answering mobile + TV is OFF)
3. Reading to your child
4. Healthy food and family mealtimes
5. Giving praise and naming good behaviour

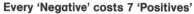

Positives, Praises and 'Attends'

→ 'attends' = paying attention to your child's attention
→ asking to play
→ describing and 'telling the story of what is happening'
→ gentle touching
→ acknowledging effort and intentions
→ praising
→ smiling with appreciation
→ imitation
→ ignoring naughtiness
→ involving child in tasks at home

Negatives

→ commands and telling a child what to do
→ teaching
→ telling off
→ criticism
→ irritated tone of voice
→ demands
→ saying 'No!'
→ negative/rough touch
→ negative non-smiling face
→ mocking, teasing
→ ignoring
→ loud voice
→ shouting

The Parent/Child Game
By Sue Jenner, Bloomsbury 2000,
ISBN 9780747596806

'Bringing up children is one of the most difficult tasks in the world – and potentially one of the most rewarding. Loving and conveying love may seem to be instinctive skills, but they can also be worked on and improved, and it is now established that parenting is not necessarily an inherent talent, but is something that can be learned. Parents need no longer feel guilty, incompetent or useless when family relationships aren't what they should be, – nor do children have to feel unloved, ignored or misunderstood. ... In her work as a clinical psychologist with families from many cultures, Sue Jenner has experienced great success with the technique known to psychologists as the 'Parent/Child Game'.'

THE
PARENT/CHILD
GAME
The Proven Key to a Happier Family
SUE JENNER

'All excellent book'
Guardian

Performing 'Tricks' or a Sense of Achievement: To clap or not to clap?

All children need praise and acknowledgement. We all do. But it is not helpful to interrupt a child's activity or concentration by clapping, or even asking him to clap for himself, each time he has correctly inserted a puzzle piece or made a mark on a paper. It adds nothing and distracts his attention. The child performs these tasks from inward motivation and does not need praise. He doesn't do it for us. He does it for himself. The child explores, plays and does things, because he knows that he needs to do it in order to learn, improve and develop himself. This is what brings him satisfaction.

Sometimes too much praise can even take away the child's own sense of satisfaction. Sometimes it makes a child feel misunderstood ('I didn't do it for YOU, I did it for myself! So stop interrupting me, mummy!'), embarrassed or even patronized. Sometimes adults clap a child, because they want to have his attention for themselves rather than allowing him to find his own satisfaction and sense of achievement. Sometimes a simple nod or sound of acknowledgement is much more appropriate than clapping or applauding, – except if he is pretending to be a performing circus-animal. We don't want him to do things in order to get applause. We want him to do it, because he WANTS to do it, because he likes doing it, because doing it brings him satisfaction, – not in order to perform for us. We want to help him to find the satisfaction of a job well done INSIDE himself.

> **'ATTENDS' ARE BETTER THAN PRAISE:**
> 'Listen to what your child is telling you (e.g. in their behaviour) about how they are feeling/thinking) and say it back to them in words.'
> (Sue Jenner)

Praise
→ A smile, a hug or a friendly nod are sometimes even better praise than words or clapping.
→ Don't praise everything, or your praise loses its meaning.
→ Give specific praise like 'Thank you for hanging up your coat.' or 'I like the way you shared that toy.'
→ 'Well done for tidying up your shoes.' is better than just 'Well done' or 'Good boy', because it tells your child, what it is you are pleased about.

Play with a Purpose

Children need Things to Play with and Something to do

When there's nothing to do and nothing to play with, children may get bored, noisy, boisterous or unhappy. Then things may go 'wrong' and children may get told off for apparently being 'naughty', when in fact they were only trying to create a game out of nothing or improve a boring situation. It is not possible to bring up a child in an impeccably clean and tidy flat without creating developmental and behavioural problems. Children who are expected to sit quietly and not make a mess, cannot develop their body and brain.

How many different structures can you build from a pack of 10 washing up sponges?

> Children need purposeful activities to do and things to explore and play with. The most valuable play materials are NOT expensive man-made toys but everyday objects with no specific purpose or function.

The washing machine as activity centre: put in, take out, add powder, hang up, sort, fold...

Helping with everyday tasks

When used as opportunities for playful interaction with adults, then all young children love to help in the house, where they can learn so many important things, including sequencing, finishing a task, as well as self-help skills:

→ **Cooking** and helping with food preparation in the kitchen: washing lentils, peeling cucumbers/potatoes, grating carrots/ cheese, shelling fresh peas or beans ...

→ **Washing up, drying up, putting away** clean cutlery and dishes, – helps also with sorting and categorising

→ **Sweeping and mopping** the floor is also great physical exercise and a satisfying task to see dirt disappear and making the floor wet first, and then nice and shiny

→ **Hoovering**, – most children love using the big hoover and making dirt disappear

→ **Washing machine**: putting in dirty washing, separating light from dark colours, emptying washing machine, hanging up washing, using the dryer, folding clean washing, matching socks, sorting each family member's clean folded clothes

→ **Cleaning** the bath, sink, other surfaces ...

Young children love to help in the kitchen, like this 2 ½ year old grating cheese

Washing up means learning about physics and maths

Rhymes and Songs

Rhymes and songs are a great way of playing with your child, both outdoors and indoors, and a wonderful way to learn language, rhythm and social skills. Here are some examples:

There are action songs and circle songs. Get some tapes or CDs from the library to learn new songs. Audio-tapes are best as they leave the imagination free for the mind to concentrate on the movements and interaction, while DVDs tend to encourage sitting down to watch others do the actions. Use them to learn the song, then switch it off.

See section on Rhymes, singing and songs in 'Playing and Autism'

Rhymes and rhythm help you to know, where the words go

Mindbuilders' Rhyme Cards 2

Rhymes to WOO a Child into Interaction and Shared Play

Sibylle Janert and Carol Mannion
www.mindbuilders-consulting.org

Card Set 1
Interactive Rhymes (FDL1-2), ISBN 978-0-9557866-2-4

Card Set 2
Cooperative Rhymes (FDL3/4), ISBN 978-0-9557866-3-1

To buy a set of Rhyme cards @ £10 +p/p , www.mindbuilders-consulting.org

Drawing

Drawing is more versatile and creative than writing, but also more direct and simple. Already a mark on paper can express something of what the child is feeling: a very faint pale line tells us something very different from a forceful bright orange scribble. Encouraging children to use pens or crayons to draw gives them the opportunity to express their ideas and feelings for us to see and share. Already very young children like scribbling games, and older children can represent how they see and experience the world in recognisable form.

Drawing comes before Copying: Imagination before Numbers and Letters

Sometimes parents are proud that their child can 'count' or recite the alphabet or numbers. But sometimes this child only recite letters or numbers. He cannot talk, and he cannot draw. Knowing letters and numbers does not help a child to talk. Children learn to talk long BEFORE they can understand letters and numbers. Sometimes children have been encouraged to copy letters and numbers in the mistaken belief that this will 'teach' them to talk. But being able to copy letters, numbers or shapes does not develop a child's own ideas and imagination.

Sharing some concentrated painting time with dad

Whoops!

Leg over, leg over,
My dog went to Dover.
He came to a stile and
'**Whoops!**' -
He went over.

*Hold child facing out on your lap, cross his feet over alternately on each word. On "**Whoops**" lift up his legs excitedly. Can also be done sitting opposite or next to each other.*

Illustration © Elaine Holt

The Golden Boat

This is the boat, the golden boat,
That sails on the silvery sea.
And these are the oars of ivory white,
That lift and dip, that lift and dip,
Here are the 10 little ferry men,
Running along, running along,
To take the oars of ivory white,
That lift and dip, that lift and dip,
That move the boat, the golden boat,
Over the silvery sea.

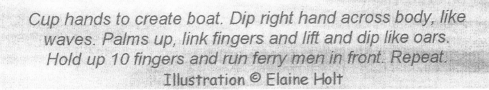

*Cup hands to create boat. Dip right hand across body, like
waves. Palms up, link fingers and lift and dip like oars.
Hold up 10 fingers and run ferry men in front. Repeat.*
Illustration © Elaine Holt

And without his own ideas a child won't have anything to talk about. Imagination and talking about one's ideas needs to come first. It is in drawing that a child discovers, what is in his mind, and finds ways to express and share it. Letters and numbers come into play once the child has a sense of his own ideas and imagination, which means they need to come AFTER the child can talk and use mark-making to show his ideas and express his feelings.

Drawing activities:

→ *Take turns doing a scribble using different crayons, pen, pencils …*

→ *The adult draws quick and simple sketches of things that the child is interested in, e.g. saying good bye, car, helicopter, bus, apple, child crying, buttons in the lift, lift doors opening and closing, pooh in the toilet ..*

→ *The adult draws quick and simple sketches of shared events that happened recently and had an emotional impact on the child, e.g. child crying when mummy left him at school, shock when ice-cream was dropped, dog in the park eating up dropped biscuit, child screaming on floor in supermarket.*

→ *The adult does the drawing with the child describing and telling the adult what to draw.*

→ *Adult and child take turns adding to a joint picture*

→ *Child draws and adult watches with interest what the child creates and tells him. Avoid asking too many questions, which can easily wreck this lovely activity. Don't be greedy. Just be interested and describe what you see.*

→ *Draw into sand by the beach or river when going for a walk using a stick.*

'Bad drawings' are helpful

Don't be afraid that you can't draw. In fact, 'bad drawings' are more helpful than perfect or machine made pictures. A quick sketch that doesn't look much like the car, person or incident you want it to represent will require more imagination and talking, as you will have to tell the child what it is supposed to be. You now have something like a shared secret for both you and your child to remember. Imperfect drawings from adults also help children not to lose confidence or feel that they can't draw as well as the adult.

Drawing together can be one of the simplest, yet most creative activities

Drawing in the sand with fingers or sticks at the beach

Family drawing session: following rhythms and sharing attention

Story telling

Story-telling is the most versatile and wonderful activity that is greatly under-used as it can be done anywhere and at any time. Apart from being a lovely shared activity, making up a story together encourages attention, listening and meaningful language skills as well as imagination, creativity and logical thinking. Of course stories can also be used to deal with difficult situations, feelings or subjects, e.g. how to respond when meeting a stranger at the bus stop or a friend, or when someone is sitting on the child's favorite seat on the bus.

Story ideas

→ Jenny has a treasure box. What do you think is inside?
→ Ahmed was sitting upstairs on a bus looking out the window when ...
→ I don't want to go to school today!
→ The duck and the cat went to the forest together ...
→ Jimmy is upset, because his dad won't allow him to kick his football in the house because of the windows. Jimmy doesn't understand why he can't play football at home. Do you?
→ We were all in the car and the policeman stopped us ...
→ You know what happened to me today?
→ In the holidays we are going to visit my ...
→ Yesterday we played a new game at school.
→ Once upon a time there was a family ...
→ Last night I had a dream ...

How?

→ *Play and act out the story together as you make it up.*
→ *Involve siblings or friends*
→ *Take turns making up sentences.*
→ *Dress up or make props*
→ *Draw the story, – the adult does the drawing with the child giving instructions*
→ *Use little people, animals or dolls to play out the story*
→ *Write the story down.*
→ *Record the story on a tape recorder or similar, and play it back. Avoid using video as this will distract from listening and creating a story.*
→ *Make a story book and write down a story every day, including date, illustration*
→ *Make up 'cloud-stories' when outdoors about different clouds: 'Look at that cloud over there: it looks like giant eating an ice-cream. Can you see it?' – 'No, that's not a giant. It's a sheep trying to catch its tail.'*

Children listening intently to a story told from a tiny back-of-a-lorry stage

WHERE?
On your lap
As a bed time story
Walking along to school
On Sundays while in the park
In the car
With a candle and the lights out on a dark rainy day
Lying in the grass in the summer looking up at the sky

One day I fell asleep on the tube. When I woke up, there was a huge bear sitting opposite me. All alone. How did it get there?

Playing outdoors and going outside every day

Children need to go outside every day. Their skin needs vitamin D that comes from daylight, even when it is not sunny, to prevent problems arising from vitamin deficiencies like bow legs or later diabetes. Their brain needs the oxygen and new experiences in order to grow the necessary brain connections. Their eyes need to see things at the distance. Their bodies need the movement from walking and running, climbing and moving about.

Children need to experience the changing seasons and how to dress for different temperatures. If you move and run, you get warm even when it is cold outside. Children living in cold climates go out every day, – they may even ski to school, which is fun! There is probably nothing more fun to play with than snow: skiing, tobogganing, sledges, snowball fights, building snow men or igloos.

In fact it is so important for human beings, that even prisoners have the right to go outdoors for at least 1 hour a day. So why are there so many children whose parents don't take them out every day?

Walk, don't drive everywhere!

Walking is very important for children as well as for adults, especially though not only in natural environments. Walking moves the whole body in a regular rhythm that has a regulating and calming function, coordinating all the parts of the body: arms, legs, feet, knees, head, eyes, brain, even the internal organs, i.e. it helps with digestion, eating difficulties and toilet training. The regular rhythm of walking regulates breathing and fresh air feeds the brain with oxygen that is needed for learning as well as for language development. Driving a child everywhere in a car misses myriads of opportunities for learning, and it inhibits growing up and becoming independent. There is so much a child can notice, learn and talk about when out walking with a parent, e.g. seeing trees and nature change over the course of the year, or about the people and things you pass in the street.

Going outdoors improves children's eyes and visual behaviour

Going outdoors is also crucial for visual maturation, as the brain needs lots of experience of moving the focus of the eyes from seeing something in the far distance to something nearby. Seeing and making sense of what we see is not an automatic process. The brain needs plenty of visual practice and experience in order to grow the neuronal pathways that result in healthy use of the eyes and visual behaviours. Many 'modern children' arrive at school 'visually immature', which can result in behavioural problems, because the child's eyes cannot adjust quickly enough between seeing what is on the

This little child feels like a prisoner. It is sunny outside. But he is stuck in a pen. What has he done wrong? Even prisoners are allowed out into the open air at least one hour every day

Without daily exercise and fresh air a child's brain and mind don't develop well, leaving a hole in the child's experience

Jumping and uneven ground requires careful coordination of body, eyes and brain

table right before him to something at the distance, like the teacher or a blackboard. Children need plenty of experience of seeing long distance, like birds or ducks at a distance, a child or a dog running towards them or playing ball in the park.

But he'll catch a cold!

No, he won't. Not if you dress him properly and play games together that involve running and moving to keep warm. You don't catch a cold from going outdoors when it is cold, – even though in English it is the same word. The common cold is a viral infection we catch from other people, not from being outdoors. People get more colds in winter precisely because they are indoors so much more: indoors people breathe stale heated air that dries up the mucous membranes and makes them more susceptible to the germs that are passed from person to person. Germs and viruses don't like the cold. They like it warm. Like indoors. With the windows shut. That's what gets children to keep catching colds. Strong temperature differences activate the immune cells thus strengthening the immune system, which is why children in Russia are taken outdoors naked in the winter to rub down with snow to build up their immunity. The germs hate it, so they don't get colds.

In fact, what most protects a child from catching colds is
→   enough sleep
→   washing hands and clean what's been touched so germs don't get passed on
→   movement, at least 30 minutes every day, makes immune cells more active, so they can fight germs better
→   going outdoors and facing, meeting or 'fighting' the cold
→   opening the windows to air your house and let in fresh air at least once a day

Children need to get outside into nature every day. There are so many different things to notice, see, hear and do discover

You don't catch a cold from going outside when it is cold. Going out to rub down with snow will make these Russian children get hot and strengthen their immune system

How about throwing stones into a pond or river and watching the ripples? Big stones, little stones, red ones, white ones ... and watch out not to get wet feet!

Some places to go to and things to do

→ Go to different playgrounds to climb, swing, slide, play in the sand …

→ Go to different parks to run, play catch or tag, throw a Frisbee, – there are so many other things you can do together, – as well as playing football

→ Climb a tree, roll down a hill, make a den, play 'tag' and hide-and-seek

→ Feed the ducks, fly a kite, collect autumn leaves or pebbles or twigs

→ Watch the birds, squirrels, – and wonder about how they live and where?

→ Fly a kite, – perhaps a simple one made from a paper or plastic bag attached to a string

→ Walking on stilts is fun, as are hoola hoops

→ Bikes, Balance bikes, scooters are great for moving forward

→ Ball games: catching and throwing, using rackets like badminton, or table-tennis in the park

→ Go to the sea side to see the tides, play in the water, feel the wind, throw stones into the water and watch the ripples, marvel at the horizon and the infinity of space

→ Take a bus and go to a different part of town

→ Take a boat to go up the river …

→ Go on a rowing boat on the lake in the park

→ Take a picnic in the summer

→ Go to the city farm, the zoo, library, airport (just for a visit to watch the planes), museum, theatre …

→ And: don't just go shopping! There are so many other interesting things to see and do and places to go to …

Spinning on a playground round-about is fun, involves interaction and stimulates certain parts of the brain

Balance bikes, also called 'Like-a'bike', help children's brains to develop their sense of balance instead of relying on stabilisers

Children need Something to Play with: Play Materials and Toys with a High Play Value

Many modern children have lots of colourful plastic toys. But parents often complain that their child doesn't really play with them. We all know the child who played more with the box and the packaging than with the actual expensive toy that was inside. Though man-made and expensive, many modern toys do not have anything like the same play-value as a cardboard box or certain 'old-fashioned' toys. In fact, there is often not very much you can do with modern toys, because they have a fixed agenda: all a child can do with press-the-button-toys is to press the buttons and let the toy 'do its thing'. There is no room to expand the toy's repertoire. These toys don't encourage genuine creativity and imagination. But are not imagination and creativity the most important thing in a child's life …?

This Bolivian mother is using a cardboard box as a kind of play-pen for her child while she works at her little store as a street-vendor

Playing with everyday, natural and recycled materials

Good toys and 'play-things' for your child do not have to cost much money. In fact there are lots of materials in every household that can be used for imaginative play with your child to encourage imagination and creativity, language and problem-solving, e.g. card-board boxes of all shapes and sizes, empty yoghurt-pots or other containers that have been washed, egg-boxes, ... With a little imagination, toilet rolls can become a chimney and wheels for a tractor, or even glasses! (see also section on 'Recycled materials' in Playing and Autism)

Natural play and everyday materials

Children love collecting things. They love to pick up and carry leaves, stones, sticks and twigs, and to show us what they have found. They also like to carry heavy things from one place to another. This helps them to achieve uprightness and to be well balanced. Even in urban environments children can collect conkers and acorns, colourful autumn leaves and beautiful stones when outdoors in the park or green spaces.

How about collecting mango, peach and apricot stones, taking them into the bath to be scrubbed, cleaned and dried, an activity that might take your child a few evenings to complete? They can be sorted, counted and moved around in a toy-truck, or become stock or 'money' when playing shops. Walnuts and other nuts are also beautiful and can be used for play before they are cracked and eaten. Pieces of wood, like off-cuts from a carpenters, make fantastic building materials.

Children need non-toy materials to play with

During the day, there must be things around that the children can use and reach by themselves to play without having to ask an adult to get it for them. This can be toys, – but more important are 'non-toys' and creative materials that only become something with the help of the child's imagination, e.g.:

→ Paper, card and card board
→ Pens, pencils and crayons
→ String, Sellotape, clothes pegs, paper-clips and other things to connect one thing to another
→ Boxes, bags, containers and empty packaging of all different shapes and sizes
→ Blankets, scarves, towels as well as big and small pieces of material that can make a house or become a teddy's blanket, a doll's nappy, shawl or sari, or a lake or a flag ...
→ Sofa cushions can become mountains or dens for toys to hide under

With the help of mum's clothes' pegs the children's slippers became a train with carriages and passengers.
Clothes pegs make great toys and require fine-motor skills and hand-eye coordination.

SOMETHING TO DO
'Sitting with nothing to do is extremely stressful for children.'
Margot Sunderland

Most people have collected conkers and shells. But have you noticed how beautiful walnuts and peach stones are? Or that mango stones are furry, if you brush them first?

The most valuable play materials are often everyday objects with no specific purpose or function, including recycling materials

Not all toys are good toys!

Children don't actually need very many toys as long as they have sufficient access to a wide variety of play materials as described above and throughout this book.

Don't limit children in the use of play materials: Because different materials were available, the children have made a lake with blue paper and pens as fences around the castle

Good toys are toys with a high play-value

Good toys are those that can be used in many different ways, thus giving them endless and high play-value. Good toys encourage the child to use their mind for problem-solving, creativity and imagination, and to develop their physical, social, interactive and symbolic skills.

Building with wooden bricks together, creating different constructions every time

Check list for good toys

multi-functional + versatile	→ NOT restricted, fixed/ right-wrong use, limited to this toy
contained/ containable	→ NOT too many bits that will easily get lost, e.g. in a box
solid/ safe	→ NOT breakable/ unsafe
replaceable	→ NOT precious/ expensive
interactive, social	→ NOT solitary, can only be played with alone
cooperative (playing together)	→ NOT competitive (I win – you win)
playful + fun	→ NOT coercive, must be done 'the right way'
creative + growth-promoting	→ NOT making time pass without being meaningful
encourages imagination	→ NOT mechanical responses, pressing button only

'Little world' figures: they almost start to create a story all by themselves

How to choose a 'Good Toy'

Questions to ask when looking for toys:

1. Are there **lots of different things to play with** this, i.e. is it multi-functional, versatile, imaginative, symbolic

2. Does it **encourage the child's imagination**, i.e. to think 'What can I (the child) do with this?'
3. Can it easily be made interactive/ sociable, i.e. **can others join in easily**?

Some examples of toys with a 'high play value'

1. **Teddies, soft animals and dolls** are very important for all children to be able to play out their own daily experiences of sleeping and eating, playing and going out, feeling loved, upset, tired, hungry or told off. Card board boxes can become beds, tables and chairs, or a bath, pram or car. They may have their own clothes or knitted jumpers, hats and shoes too.

2. **Wooden Bricks or Blocks**, in plain colours and without any letters or numbers on them, are among the best toys a child can have, as there are endless possibilities for play. Wooden bricks are best, because you can do more with them than with any other toy. However, it is very important that they should be 'just bricks', i.e. not also try to 'teach numbers and letters', which will only serve to distract the child from using his own ideas and imagination. Just make sure you have enough bricks (about 100) and a solid container to store them in, like a box with a lid.

3. **Little Play People and Animal Families** should be part of every city-child's play-equipment, so he can re-play his everyday experiences to help him to think and build his mind. Playmobil people are good, because they can stand up and move their arms and legs.

4. **Plasticine** is more versatile because it is both harder than Play Dough and lends itself better to making small symbolic things from it.

5. **Construction games** such as Lego, marble runs, Meccano, ... that allow the child to make and construct things. Duplo is good for small children, but I would avoid the cheap version of large plastic ricks that stick together. They have only a very limited play-value, because the bricks are too big and there are never enough to really create a proper house or car ...

6. **Board games** and other games with rules, such as Lotto-games, 'Snakes and Ladders', ...

Sorting and tidying up:
Everything needs to have a home!
Every evening, and every now and again during the day, it will be time to tidy up and put things 'where they belong', which is another very important activity of picking up and letting go, sorting, categorizing for learning to communicate, think, talk and problem-solve.

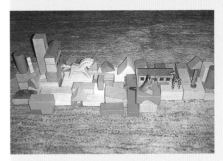
This complex construction with bricks and wooden animals started as a removal van moving house. Later that day, it became a boat and by the evening it was an island in the middle of the ocean

Play materials with 'high play value', like plasticine, encourage creativity, interaction, cooperation, communication and imagination

Marble-runs are great toys requiring imagination and negotiation as well as testing out ideas through trial and error

Look at the pictures together and help your child to make sense of them. Children need to be able to talk about the pictures before looking at the writing on the page

Picture Books

Children love picture books, and so do most adults! There is so much to see and talk and think about. Picture books open ever new worlds to children and opportunities to share ideas, talk about the pictures or to study them on one's own.

For healthy language development it is important that your child can make sense of the pictures and talk with you about the story, long before he get ready or even interested in reading the text and the words. Children need to be confident in talking about the pictures and the ideas in their head, before they can meaningfully learn to read. When looking at picture-books with a young child,

→ focus on talking ABOUT the pictures and the book's STORYLINE,

→ enjoy the RHYTHM of simple storybooks that describe what the pictures show, e.g. Hairy Macleary books

→ ask OPEN QUESTIONS showing you are interested in what your child sees and thinks, – and avoid tedious 'vocabulary tests' of constantly questioning a young child 'What's this? What's that?'

→ LOOK together at the pictures rather than just reading the words/text!

This boy is pointing out something very important to his mum, who is paying such good attention ... that she is almost spilling her tea!

LOOKING at pictures and picture books

There are really 3 key elements to reading/looking at picture-books with a child:

1. *the story on the page,*
2. *the story in the book, i.e. the sequence of what happens between the pages*
3. *the main idea, i.e. 'What's this book about?', which is central to being in mainstream-school.*

Listening to the rhythm of grandma reading a story, the child begins to understand the story on the page and the story of the whole book

Looking at picture books together helps with

→ Focusing, paying attention and concentrating
→ Looking + listening to soft tones of voice and rhythmic repetitions of parent reading
→ Sitting down and staying in one place for a while
→ Self-regulation, staying organised and calm
→ Sharing attention and enjoying each other's company
→ Recognising, remembering, looking for and finding pictures again
→ Linking everyday experiences to pictures and sounds/ words
→ Emotional engagement, turn-taking and relationships
→ Initiating interaction, e.g. showing each other pictures
→ Recognising pictures, naming and pointing
→ Copying + stringing together several gestures, sounds and words
→ Sharing ideas + giving you something to talk about with each other

Bolivian girls sharing books and stories with each other

Going to the library

Libraries are great because they allow the child to look at a wide range of books, to learn to choose, to take and to return, as well as an opportunity to read and look at new books. It is very helpful to make regular weekly visits into part of your family routine, e.g. every Thursday after school, to your local library. Take out 3 books each time for each child, so you can enjoy the variety as well as trying out what your child likes, and what is and isn't suitable for your child at the moment.

Libraries are great places to go and visit regularly with your child

Some recommended picture books
Children under 3 years
Look for

→ **simple realistic pictures** (i.e. photos or realistic draw-ings, – avoid comic-like pictures, which are more difficult for young children to recognise and make sense of) of
→ **everyday situations** like in the park, at home, eating, going to the shops, having a bath, school, etc. and
→ with a very **simple story-line** and
→ lots of **rhythm** and **repetition**

First books give the child a surprise or something to do
→ Lift the flap books, e.g. Spot books
→ Touch-and-Feel books (but NOT press-the-button 'books', or 'books' with batteries)

Making personal photo-books

Making personal photo-books is a great activity for every child with endless potential for conversation:

Take some photos of situations that are important to the child and make them into personal photo-books to encourage conversation and story-telling together. Focus on emotionally significant situations, interactions and people doing things, so you can share memories and talk about what happened and what he was feeling. Avoid staged photos of objects of people just smiling into the camera, as they don't usually give you much to talk about apart from 'oh, that's nice'. Little mishaps and unusual moments are particularly good, as they have emotional significance. Make different books to different themes, include 'first – then' pictures, e.g.

A personal photo-book helps this boy to communicate and to share his ideas with other people

1. **At home:** pictures of mum cooking, then everyone having dinner together, dad getting into car, mum waving good bye, someone hoovering, child sleeping in his bed, playing the piano, helping mum do the washing up, fill/empty the washing machine, dad/mum being cross with someone, little sister crying, ...

2. **At weekends:** pictures of child and dad in the park, getting into/out of car, playing with mum, ...

Although electronic devices can be helpful in this, a small photo-album allows for more calming conversations about the pictures, than electronic devices with their seductive pull to becoming absorbed in flicking and clicking

3. **Other places:** pictures of school from the outside, inside; at sports club; swimming; in the supermarket pushing the trolley; at the dentist, in doctor's waiting room; at the train station; at a friend's house; at the zoo; at the farm; at the airport, ...

4. **Other people:** pictures of familiar people doing things, e.g. family members, relatives from abroad, staff and children from school, ... Try to get photos of these people 'in action', and not just smiling into the camera, which makes it difficult to find things to talk about. Ideally try to get photos of typical activities, e.g. granddad smoking his pipe, mum going to work, uncle the bus driver washing his bus, ...

5. **Outings:** do a specific outing and take shots of different moments and things you did that the child particularly enjoyed or that aroused strong emotions (surprise, fear, anger, ...) , e.g. going to the zoo or an animal park, indoor play center, ice skating, funfair, ...

6. **Holidays + festivals:** pictures of events and people doing things, e.g. Christmas, Easter, birthdays, summer holidays, Halloween, tobogganing, swimming, horse riding, ...

Some Recommended Picture Books

Title	Author	Publisher	ISBN
Nursery Rhymes			
Playtime Rhymes + CD	Sally Gardner	Orion	072860887
Nursery Rhymes	Michael Foreman		0744598206
The Usborne Book of Nursery Rhymes + CD	C. Hooper	Usborne	0746057407
The Orchard Book of Nursery Rhymes	Faith Jaques	Orchard	978 1 85213 056 5
The Orchard Book of Nursery Rhymes for your baby	Penny Dann	Orchard	978 1 40830 458 7
First Rhymes	Lucy Coates	Orchard	978 1 86039 419 5
Rhymes for Annie Rose	Shirley Hughes	Red Fox	0099464918
Early books			
Cock-A-Moo-Moo	Julie Dallas-Conte /Alison Bartlett	Macmillan	0333947533
Time to get dressed	Elivia Savadier	Roaring Brook Press	159643161X
Can you moo moo too?	David Wojtowycz	Orchard	978 1 40831 228 5
Can you choo choo too?	David Wojtowycz	Orchard	978 1 40831 227 8
What we do	Reg Cartwright	Hutchinson	0091884969
A Teeny Tiny Baby	Amy Schwartz	Roaring Brook Press	1596431938
Please, baby, please	Spike Lee	Simon & Schuster	0689834578
Eat up, Gemma	Sarah Hayes	Walker	1406306703
Let's have fun	Verna Wilkins	Tamarind	1870516540
Rhyming stories and Rhymes			
We're going on a bear hunt	Michael Rosen	Walker	9781406319408
Brown bear, brown bear, what do you see?	Bill Martin Jr/Eric Carle	Puffin	0141501596
Polar bear, polar bear, what do you hear?	Bill Martin Jr/Eric Carl	Puffin	0141383518
The Seals on the bus	Lenny Hort	Henry Holt	0805086781
Whoever you are	Mem Fox	Harcourt	0152060308
Bedtime Stories			
Good Night, Moon	Margaret Wise Brown	Macmillans	0230748600
Good night, Harry	Kim Lewis	Walker	1844285006
Hush, little Polar Bear	Jeff Mack	Roaring Brook Press	978-1596433687
Little Night	Yuyi Morales	Roaring Brook Press	978-1596430884
At Night	Jonathan Beans	Farrar Straus Giroux	978-0374304461
Lets go to bed	Verna Wilkins	Tamarind	1870516559
Alex Ayliffe			
Go Baby! My day: Mealtime		Orchard	978 1 40831 504 0
Go Baby! My day: Playtime		Orchard	978 1 40831 505 7
Go Baby! My day: Bathtime		Orchard	978 1 40831 502 6
Go Baby! My day: Bedtime		Orchard	978 1 40831 503 3

Trish Cooke

So much	Walker	1406306657
Full full full of love	Walker	1844287823

Lynly Dodd

Hairy Maclary from Donaldson's Dairy	Puffin	0670913502
Hairy Maclary, sit	Puffin	0141330953
Hairy Maclary, shoo	Puffin	0141328061
Hairy Maclary and Zachary Quack	Puffin	0141381132
Zachary Quack Minimonster	Puffin	0141500395
Slinky Malinky	Puffin	0140544399
Slinky Malinky, Open the door	Puffin	0141381140
Slinky Malinky Catflaps	Puffin	0140565728
Slinky Malinky's Christmas Crackers	Puffin	014150109X

Shirley Hughes

Out and About	Walker	9781844284733
Don't want to go	Red Fox	1862306702
Alfie's World	Bodley Head	0370328949
All about Alfie	Bodley Head	037033194X
Alfie's feet	Red Fox	1862307849
Annie Rose is my little sister	Red Fox	0099408562
Alfie gives a hand	Red Fox	1862307857
Alfie and the big boys	Red Fox	0099488442
Olly and Me: Hiding	Walker	1844284719
Olly and Me: Bouncing	Walker	1844284700
Olly and Me: Giving	Walker	1844285308
Olly and Me: Chatting	Walker	1844285294
Olly and Me: Colours	Walker	0744569818
Olly and Me: Noisy	Walker	0744569834
Olly and Me: Bathwater is hot	Walker	0340378247

Jill Murphy

Peace at last	Campbell	0333712773
Five minutes Peace	Walker	9781406330120
Mr. Large in Charge	Walker	9781406320961
The last Noo Noo	Walker	9780744598353
A Piece of Cake	Walker	9781844285266
The Large Family: Collection	Walker	9780744582284

Helen Oxenbury

Tom and Pippo's Day	Walker	0689712766
Tom and Pippo go for a walk	Walker	0689712545
Tom and Pippo go shopping	Walker	0689712782
Tom and Pippo read a Story	Walker	0744510287
Tom and Pippo make a friend	Walker	0744512700
Pippo gets lost	Walker	0689819579
Tom and Pippo and the Washing Machine	Walker	0689712553

Martin Waddell

Owl Babies		Walker	074454923x
Sleep tight, little bear		Walker	9780744540673
Can't you sleep, little bear?		Walker	9781844284917

Longer stories

Where the wild things are	Maurice Sendak	Red Fox	0099408392
Dogger	Shirley Hughes	Red Fox	1862308055
Not now, Bernard	David McKee	Red Fox	0099240505
Tell me the day backwards	Albert Lamb	Walker	9781406331684
Harry's Home	L+C Anholt	Orchard	978 1 40830 215 6
Going to Nursery	L+C Anholt	Orchard	978 1 40830 211 8
Sophie and the New Baby	L+C Anholt	Orchard	978 1 40830 213 2
There's going to be a baby	John Burningham	Walker	9780744549966
My friend Harry	Kim Lewis	Walker	0744552958
A New Year's Reunion	Yu Li-Qiong	Walker	9781406337327
Vera's First Day at School	Vera Rosenberry	Owlet Book	978-0805072693
Going home	Eve Bunting	Joanna Cotler Books	0060262974

4 Playing and AUTISM

What is Autism?

Autism is a Relationship Disorder
→ of variable severity, ranging from mild to severe difficulties
→ also referred to as Autistic Spectrum Disorder/Condition, ASD/ASC, autistic features/behaviours, on the spectrum
→ is multi-causational, i.e. the result of a combination of many different factors coming together in unfortunate ways
→ includes communication difficulties, – and some children don't learn to speak, while others never stop
→ with puzzling/ challenging behaviours
→ often linked with difficulties with sensory-motor processing and making sense of their perceptions (seeing, hearing/listening, touch, movement, ...)
→ which affects early mental development and making sense of the world and people
→ due to an impairment of the ordinary sense of emotional curiosity about and desire for relationships, i.e. relating to the other person more as a source of sensory stimulation than as a human being with feelings and ideas

Other Facts about Autism
→ Diagnosis of autism/ autistic spectrum disorder/ASD is increasing world-wide
→ Almost 20% of young children are diagnosed in UK with an Autistic Spectrum Disorder/ASD (Baird 2004)
→ About 1-2 of every 100 primary school children in the UK diagnosed as autistic/ASD (NAS 2008)
→ There are countless different approaches and theories about autism
→ Parents often complain about ending up with conflicting advice by autism-professionals
→ Local authorities face spiraling costs, as many autistic children cannot cope in mainstream school
→ Only very few places at expensive special schools (costing between £30.000 – £200.000 per year per child)
→ There are not enough services: especially early intervention and post-diagnosis support, but also in day care and residential provision for children and adults with autism

The word 'autism' describes a child who finds communicating with other people difficult

The puzzling autistic behaviours are often due to sensory processing differences

Diagnosis of autism is increasing world-wide

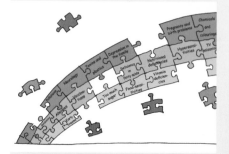

Autism seems to be the result of a combination of many different factors coming together in unfortunate ways

What we don't know about Autism
One Word – Many Meanings

Despite the fact that there is one single word/ term, which seems to suggest that we know what 'autism' is, there is however no clear overall agreement what 'autistic' really is and what exactly different people mean when talking about 'autism' or 'autistic spectrum disorder'.

The controversy is around
a) What exactly is the nature of the core impairment?
b) Where is the core damage located, – in the brain or in the mind?

Autism in the Family

Because of the severity of the condition, with autism it is never just the child who is affected, but the whole family, thus making parent-focused early intervention programs crucial.

AUTISM OR AUTISMS? There are probably many different kinds of autisms

We don't know whether the core problem of autism is in the brain or in the mind

Autism in the Family
Sibylle Janert
in collaboration with Sheila Coates and Merete Hawkins
Illustrations: Claudia Schenk

Autism in the Family:
Picture-book for adults and siblings
By Sibylle Janert, Sheila Coates, Merete Hawkins, 2006, ISBN 0955786606

This book is meant for sharing. It aims to inspire you to think about autism and how we can reach out and connect with a child with autistic behaviours: parents, siblings, other family members, professionals. Specially designed to be accessible to all families and including those, who often miss out on crucial early intervention, because the relatively new diagnostic category of ASD is still unknown in their language/culture or who don't read or speak English well, the idea is that talking about the pictures with each other will stimulate thinking and help with understanding.

'Autism in the Family' aims to
→ bring together parents, siblings and others to talk and think about autism
→ be accessible for those who prefer pictures to reading books
→ lighten the trauma of diagnosis
→ proposes a more optimistic prognosis for autistic spectrum disorder/ASD
→ illustrate a modern social approach to autism
→ provide a 'talking point' between parents and others working with autism, including Diagnostic Teams, Children's Centres, Paediatricians, Early Years and Social Services

9b   AUTISM is NOT 'mad' or 'bad' or 'stupid' or 'naughty' or 'possessed by evil spirits', Autism is NOT 'just a speech-problem', NOT the mother's fault and NOT a punishment from above. Autism is a disorder of early mental development.

Social Approaches to Autism

There are many approaches to autism. These can roughly be divided into 2 main groups, – with the biological approaches trying to address symptoms by bio-chemical and physical interventions, while the educational-therapeutic approaches focus on the child's learning and development:

1. The behavioural approaches focus on teaching and trained skills and behaviours, and include ABA (Applied behaviour analysis), PECS (Picture Exchange Communication System), TEACCH (Training and Education for ...), Makaton sign language, and others.

2. Social approaches are developmental approaches that are child-centred and play-based and include the Son Rise programmes from the Options Institute, Intensive Interaction, Floortime including the PLAY-Project, which inform the activities described in this book.

It is the emotionality in the contact which can draw a child out of their cut-off state of mind into meaningful reciprocal human relationship, and their parents too

'The way you know, that you are playing at the right level, is if everyone is having fun.' Dr. Solomon

Behavioural	Play-based
Medical/Machine Model	*Relationship/ Growth Model*
Highly prescribed	*Strategic, flexible +*
More controlled	*individualised*
Programme oriented	*More naturalistic + responsive*
Led by programme goals	*Child initiated*
	Follows child's lead
Behavioural analysis	
Focus: Behaviour	*Developmental analysis*
Teaching drills & skills	*Focus: Feelings/emotional/ affect*
	Play interaction
Strategic reinforcements	
Prescribed intensity	
Perseverations: to be stopped	*Natural/ social reinforcements*
	Flexible intensity
Parents as program facilitators	*Perseverations: seen as useful*
	Parents as play-partners

Ricki G. Robinson, M.D., M.P.H.

Foreword by Stanley I. Greenspan, M.D.

Autism Solutions

How to Create a Healthy and Meaningful Life for Your Child

INNOVATIVE STRATEGIES FOR DEVELOPING THE RIGHT TREATMENT PLAN

New ways of understanding and making sense of autism by paediatrician Dr. Ricki Robinson, Harlequin, ISBN-10: 0373892098

'The way you know that you are playing at the right level, is when everyone is having a good time!' Dr. Solomon

There is Hope! Autism does not have to be a Hopeless Condition.

Proponents of a social approach to autism like the Floortime Foundation, The PLAY Project, the Options Institute, Mind-Builders and others are much more optimistic about autism and the potential of ASD-children for emotional and social growth than what we are told in the media, the web or even many professionals. Doctors tend to say that they don't want to raise false hopes in parents. But are pessimism and discouragement really more realistic than hope and encouragement? After all: there is always something that can be done. You will find lots of ideas and activities in the next pages.

As Raun Kaufmann, a trainer of parents with an autistic child and once a severely autistic little boy himself, says: 'How is a life-sentence better than an out-stretched hand or an open door?'

Greenspan (2003, 2006) and his team of Floortime practitioners say: If we can offer the young autistic child intensive attention that focuses on relationship-building and the development of his sense of self, through interactive and playful interventions with parents at home and based on
→ the child's individual differences and special interests
→ his sensory-motor strengths and weaknesses
→ each family's special patterns,
→ then about 50% of these children are ready to 'take off' and make good progress.

Parents are the most important agents for change

Parents are the natural experts on their children (Schopler & Mesibov, 1995) and therefore the logical and most important agents for change. Where parents are actively involved with their child at home and receive sufficient guidance and support that comes early enough and is well enough informed, all children can make a lot of progress. Many can even join a much more 'normal' developmental path provided sensitive help
→ comes early enough
→ is intensive enough
→ uses interactive joyful play
→ with parents in attentive 1-1 interaction
→ at home and before full-time school/ group-care
→ in a well-organised thoughtful home-environment

But 'if the child is not helped to find manageable, rewarding interactions, he or she will begin to 'shut down' the baffling environmental input and a form of self-imposed sensory deprivation will begin to set in.' (Greenspan 1998). www.floortime.org, www.playproject.org

Many parents experience the autism diagnosis like a traumatic blow.

There is always a lot that can be done, especially when parents are actively involved and supported.

The symptoms are not the problem, but rather the child's attempt at solving their problems.

Where parents are supported in learning how to play and communicate more effectively with their child at home, children can make a lot of progress.

In Dr. Solomon's experience about 70% of children diagnosed with ASD could make 'significant progress or even recover fully, IF parents spend 15 hours/week playing with their child and IF we can show them what to do', says Dr. Rick Solomon (2007), who created the PLAY-Project in Ann Arbor, a DIR-Floortime approach that is becoming increasingly popular.

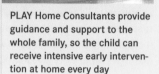

Reaching the Young Autistic Child

Reclaiming
Non-Autistic Potential
Through Communicative
Strategies and Games

Sibylle Janert

Reaching the Young Autistic Child Reclaiming Non-Autistic Potential Through Communicative Strategies and Games
A Practical Resource-Book for Parents, Nursery-Workers, Teachers And Others Working With Under-Fives

by Sibylle Janert , Free Association Books, 2000, ISBN 1 85343 498 1 9

A collection of useful ideas, activities, strategies and games developed by the author from her many years of experience of working with young children with autistic features.

PLAY Home Consultants provide guidance and support to the whole family, so the child can receive intensive early intervention at home every day

It manages to reassure the reader that autism is difficult and complex and it is ok to feel frustrated and inadequate in trying to communicate with this group of youngsters
This book gently encourages different approaches and new interactive strategies.'

Parents' sense of helplessness when faced with their child's unresponsiveness is often overwhelming and needs addressing in a practical way. This book offers encouragement and sheds light on some of these difficult issues and feelings. It aims to help all those involved with autistic children to recover, little by little, from the trauma and despair engendered by the diagnosis 'autistic', 'autistic spectrum disorder', 'autistic features', 'autistic tendencies' or 'Aspergers Syndrome'.

TV-Addiction and the Problem with Electronics and 'Press-the-button Toys'[1]

We have become an electronics and TV-culture, and many people have the TV on all day and/or spend hours in front of computers, mobiles or other electronic devices. Everyone does. The autistic child wanting to watch TV or play with mobile or computer all day seems to be just like any other 3-year-old. Parents often see this with relief. Surely, he too will learn something from watching TV, videos or computer games? But then doubts begin to creep in. He never talks

TV-junkie having a 'sight-sound bath', – the opposite of using his mind for thinking and communicating

about it. It does not seem to affect him. He does not play-act what he has seen like his age-mates, or he plays nothing else. He only wants to see the same video. On closer inspection, it actually looks like some kind of addiction.

Is watching TV/videos wasting your child's developmental time?

Because of the autistic child's difficulties with communication and making sense of perceptions, his experience of what goes on in a screen is likely to be very different from ours. If he is unable to pull his senses together into one single meaningful focus, then whatever he is watching will not make sense. If it does not make sense, then we are faced with the serious question: what is he getting out of this passive 'activity'?

Battery-operated press-the-button and flashy-noisy toys

Battery-operated flashy-noisy toys too seem to have a particular attraction and an almost hypnotic effect. But although the child may look blissfully happy when absorbed in their lights and sounds, they do not in fact stimulate his thinking and they do not help his mind to grow, – and in fact they just make time pass unused, leading to play-deprivation and starving his mind from learning from and with other people.

The sight-and-sound bath

Making sense of the story-line in a film, although so immediate and natural to you and me, is really a complicated mental process, which is impossible without a good grasp of speech and comprehension. Essentially it requires the ability and the desire to make sense of things, to understand what things 'mean' and to let them affect us, – the autistic child's blind spots. But what is left of the TV or video experience, if we take away the story-line and the meaning of what is said and shown on the screen? A purely sensuous sight-sound-experience, a 'sight-and-sound-bath': a constantly changing colourful display of movement with an ongoing noise-background of patterns of sound or tunes.

The tranquiliser function of TV/video

But without meaningful seeing, there will be little learning. Most young autistic children do not learn much from watching TV or video. They use the 'sight-sound bath' to envelop, to wash over them in a comforting way allowing them to cut off, to let themselves drift off passively. Surrendering to that sensual and essentially mindless experience means that much of their mental functioning is switched off, with brain-activity, and learning, probably minimal. Periodically, his attention is activated by the catchy attention-grabbing jingle of advertisements, before ebbing off again into the more soothing, or hypnotic, lullaby-like flow of sounds.

Addicted to mobile phones and other electronic screens, – instead of engaging in human interaction.

The flashing lights and tingly tunes of flashy-noisy toys feel exciting to a young child, pulling him deeper into his solitary comfort zone.

An experiment for you to try

With the TV on, focus your eyes into the far distance, so that your vision becomes blurred and your awareness dispersed. Focus your attention instead on the patterns of movement on the screen and let these drift past you without trying to make sense of them or matching them to what is going on in the story. It is possible to listen to the patterns of sound without listening to the meaning of the words, just letting yourself be carried away by the ongoingness of the rhythms and the music of the sound-patterns. Letting the world go by in this way, as if nothing to do with you, creates a timeless experience, – bathing in the sensations of sight and sound, a 'video-shower'.

'The box' is uncommunicative: Is it autistic?

In some ways, the TV and other electronics reflect precisely what the autistic child thinks of life and communication: a barrage of sensory stimulations, of sights and sounds that have nothing to do with him, do not affect him, go on entirely according to their own agenda, without regard for what he is doing and feeling. In this sense it is as if 'the box' is just as uncommunicative (and autistic?) as the autistic child: neither engages in a dialogue with the world around them, both are unresponsive and expect no responsiveness from their environment (including interactive TV). A video can be seen as just as echolalic as the echolalic autistic child, echoing fragments of text and undigested, indigestible, bits of language. Both need a thoughtful alert person to make sense of what goes on. The autistic child needs the help of a sensitive adult, who can inject moments of meaningfulness, and regulate the amount and quality of TV he watches.

1(Excerpt from 'Reaching the young autistic child')

The TV talks a lot. It makes exciting sounds. But doesn't listen, understand or respond. Like an autistic child?

> Not being able to speak is not the same as not having anything to say.

'If only he'd talk, he'd be alright!'

That 'he doesn't talk' seems to be the most obvious difference between the child diagnosed with autism and his age-mates, and parents often hope: 'if only he'd talk, he'd be alright!' Teaching someone to say some words seems easy. But while some children diagnosed with ASD do begin to use words and spoken language, others never learn to talk. Is something wrong with his mouth, throat, teeth or tongue? Is the teaching-method at fault? Should the adult persist with her training, – or what's going on?

He may not have words. But we understand how he feels, because gestural and body language make up 70% , and words only 7% of human communication

WARNING!

Don't say 'say'

Asking child to say words or make sounds for you does not help them to learn language. On the contrary, it can have the opposite effect and spoil it for both of you, because he'll be likely to turn away from you and withdraw from your shared game or communication. Speaking and using language comes from having something to say and knowing someone is listening who is truly interested and wants to hear it. Take the pressure off and don't say 'say'!

Being able to imitate words is not talking

All communicative language-development must follow the same pattern. Before speech can develop, the child must have become a good communicator without words. Without being able to communicate, words have no meaning. Without meaning they have no communicative value. And some people use sign-language just as effectively to communicate and 'talk', because they, or their parents, are deaf. So: just because he doesn't talk, doesn't mean that he has nothing to say!

After all, we all use body-language including nodding, looking or hand-gestures, tone of voice and intonation to communicate, – and babies spend the first 15 months using only such non-verbal communication.

Parents often complain that the autistic child should have daily sessions with a trained speech/language therapist. But even a trained speech-therapist cannot teach him to talk! Even if he can say some words, this does not mean that he will use them, or even that he understands what they mean. He needs first to catch up with the basics of communication, necessary for all subsequent language-development. These develop only in interaction with another human being, and out of the baby's early communicativeness that needs no words.

→ Language was not 'invented' or taught, but evolved as an emergent property of the mind.
→ One's mother-tongue or first language can not be taught: it grows from the inside out in loving and nurturing relationships.
→ Human language develops through loving interactions and meaningful connections with other people.
→ In order to learn to talk a baby needs a main carer who is attuned to the baby's level of understanding and talks to him 'as if' he understands already.
→ Babies need the repeated experience of being a 'powerful communicator' already in order to 'discover' words.
→ Being able to count or recite letters does not help a child to have a meaningful interaction with other people.
→ Language develops only once basic mental properties have formed in the child's mind that allow him to 'discover' language for and inside of himself. (i.e. 'General Understanding': see 'Functional Learning').
→ Language requires the child to first be confident in communicating emotionally and non-verbally through gestures.

Speech therapists can't give a child speech, because spoken language is the tip of an iceberg. Most human communication is hidden below the surface as non-verbal gestural communication.

The key to how children learn to talk is talking with them.

Babies spend their first 18 months developing their gestural and body language to become effective communicators about their feelings and what they have in mind.

Children without speech do not 'automatically' acquire language, once they go to nursery or school

→ Language isn't just something external we put on, like a hat or a jacket.

→ Language is a vehicle for transporting one's mental images and ideas into the mind of another person.

→ Language is part of a child's way of making sense of the world and identity.

Being able to say the ABC or 'count' to 10 is not talking

→ A parrot can be taught to do this, – but it won't get him talking.

→ Talking is having a conversation and sharing ideas, not echoing letters or numbers.

→ Talking starts with the child pointing to show you something, e.g. a picture and linking this with sound-effects like vehicle/ animal sounds.

It's not only being able to say words, that is important. What is important is

→ being interested and understanding about the world

→ wanting to communicate and relate to other people

→ being able to use gestures/sounds/words to make yourself understood and express what you mean

What Needs to Happen in the Child's Mind for Speech to Develop?

Human language is not just a learnt behaviour, but consists of complex social communications about emotional/ mental states, thoughts and ideas using symbols, representations and cultural meanings.

Shared attention

When a child begins to speak, words take their place alongside other communicative gestures he is already fully fluent with. It can not be the other way round, just as one cannot paint a house before it is built. The very beginnings of language lie in the moments when a mother follows with her eyes what her baby is looking at and joins him in this. For a long time, the adult needs to home in to whatever the child, or baby, is interested in, i.e. to follow the 'contents of his mind', his intentions and ideas. A child can only learn to speak and use language, once he has a firm understanding of the importance, and the joys, of such a mutual focus on a common topic, of 'shared attention'. In a way, mother and baby are having a 'looking-conversation': the baby's silent eye-pointing may be a question that says 'Can you see what I am looking at?'. His mum may answer with 'Yes! It's a butterfly! A lovely butterfly! Oops! Gone! Where is it gone?' All of this is the beginning of 'social referencing', required for all meaningful interaction.

Talking starts with a child pointing to show you something, because he wants to share his idea with you

Using body language and gestures, this boy is sharing his ideas and feelings about a beautiful statue in the park

Looking at the other person's face to see what they are thinking and feeling is an essential pre-verbal language skill for speech to develop

Understanding how the world works

Without understanding how the world works, the child's mind cannot build the necessary structures for thinking and language. It is only by 'learning from experience', by actively exploring and experimenting that young children can begin to make sense of and to build a picture of their internal world. Where children are deprived of active exploration of a rich and stimulating environment, for whatever reason, they may not be able to learn to talk, because talking is the expression of what is emotionally meaningful to us. Some children may not explore their environment because of physical or mental challenges, others because of a lack of play-materials to explore, lack of encouragement or too much passive distraction from the flickering of electronics, like computers, mobiles, videos and TV. But all of these children can learn, if we provide them with the play-materials that build up their 'general understanding' of the world, as described in 'Every child can learn.'

Understanding of the world includes knowing where to place knives, forks and spoons when laying the table.

Social referencing

In this way the baby gradually comes to understand that what he is looking at has meaning for his mum too, and she calls it 'butterfly'. He comes to love sharing attention like that, and he wants to know what she thinks of things. He checks her face to see whether something is safe or dangerous, allowed or not, bringing a smile or a frown as response. This is called 'social referencing', the next stage on from 'shared attention'. This is what autistic children find so very difficult, or fail to establish, and where the roots are for their not having learnt to talk. This is where we have to apply our nurturing, our most focussed attention, because without these foundations all other efforts will have little meaning and effect.

Father and son enjoy a dialogue-game: by looking at each other's eyes and facial expressions they are trying to discover, what the other has in mind, and might do or say next.

Communicative Intent

Most crucial for a child to learn language is that the adult firmly believes in the child's communicative intent, i.e. being so focussed on the child, that one interprets and responds to all his actions, gestures and vocalisations as if they were a clear message: to see everything the child does, even the tiniest movements, as deliberate messages from him (even if they aren't!), all his utterances at least an attempt at communication, and to follow the child's eyes to see what he has in mind and what he could mean, i.e. 'follow the contents of his mind'.

WANTING to Communicate

Like every other child, the autistic child needs to learn to have a good time being, or mucking about, with another person. If it's fun and linked to his inner feelings (affect), then he'll want more. If he wants more, he'll ask for it, – and asking for something is communication. At that moment he will be

'Sh! The dollie is sleeping!' Using gestures with communicative intent this little girl tells us about her ideas and makes us understand.

communicating, because he wants to, not because you are telling him. He will have a 'good feel' about communicating and saying 'Hi!', because it makes him feel nice and warmly connected with another person. A child who does not communicate, does not need to learn to say words, – he needs to learn to want to communicate. If he does not want to communicate, he will not speak, even if he did have the words and language to say it. And if he did want to communicate, but could not speak (like the deaf child), he would point to things, using eye-contact and gestures to try to make you understand what he has in mind. Our aim must be to show him that communicating with another person is fun.

Gestural communication

Long before a child learns to speak, i.e. for at least his first 15 months, he communicates by

→ GESTURE: using his hands, fingers, pointing, giving, reaching, pushing away, ...
→ BODY LANGUAGE: moving his foot to say 'do it again', shrugging his shoulder, tilting his head, turning his body away/ towards you, ...
→ EYE and FACIAL expressions: smiles, laughter, frowns, focusing with interest, surprise faces, ... and most importantly different
→ TONES OF VOICE to communicate a wide range of subtle feelings and emotions including like/dislike, interest, fear, disgust, anger, frustration, sadness, greediness, love, hurt, admiration, jealousy, regret, generosity, ...

Gestural non-verbal language is in fact for speech what soil is for the tree to grow in, making up more than 90% of communication: when people are talking to each other, words make up less than 10% of their communication! Without well functioning gestural language we are therefore likely to end up with robotic speech like a computer, or as in some forms of echolalia or 'scripting' from autistic children. So: respond to your child's GESTURAL LANGUAGE and don't say 'SAY ...'!'

The child's gestures are his meaning

→ A child's gestures and what he is looking at are his language. That's how he is telling you what is in his mind.
→ He is talking to you in gestures: you can see his intention and ideas through his gestures.
→ Turn the child's gestures into words, i.e. let him hear HIS gestures and ideas spoken in YOUR words.
→ Sprinkle 'no talking dust' on your playful interactions with gesture, body, facial expressions and tone of voice....

How to understand your child:

1. *Look at what the child is looking at. Watch his eyes.*
2. *Act on what is in the environment around him.*
3. *Do what you usually do with objects (i.e. don't put the cup upside down).*
4. *Do what makes sense.*

This boy uses gestural communication, when showing his mum the picture to share his idea

Then he tells me 'It's a ball.' Is it a real word?
1. Must have the same meaning every time
2. Used with intention to communicate
3. Used flexibly across contexts

Joint attention

Joint Attention is the process of sharing one's experience of observing an object or event, by following someone else's gaze or pointing gestures. It is the mental progression from a two-some to a three-some, from 2-tracked to 3-tracked thinking. During the first 8 months a baby interacts with one 'other', i.e. he can either interact with another person OR with a toy, but not with both. This is called 'shared attention'.

Around 9 months something very exciting and fundamental happens: the baby becomes able to combine interacting with another person ABOUT an object, i.e. to play together with another person with a toy. The baby can now imagine that mum too has ideas in her mind just like he does, and he is aware that they are different, so he has to show her what his ideas are about a toy, because otherwise she won't know. This is called 'joint attention' and absolutely crucial for social development, language acquisition, cognitive development, mental health and much more.

Pointing is a child's first sentence

Pointing to show somebody something is not just stretching out a finger. This kind of pointing is much more complex, – requiring the same underlying structures as a grammatically correct sentence. Stretching out a finger only becomes 'pointing' when there are 2 people and one wants to show the other something important, which is called 'joint attention'. Joint attention pointing is an intentional act to share meaning and so complex that animals can't do it: only humans can draw the attention of another person to what they are seeing in order to share the meaning this has for them. Human children start pointing around the age of 12 months. But many children with autism have problems with pointing because it requires a shared understanding of the world and what things mean to other people as well as the communicative intent of wanting to share ideas with others.

Decorating a gingerbread house together: sharing each other's ideas and taking turns.

Sharing a joke and being able to enjoy someone else's enjoyment is an important milestone of language development.

The boy's pointing finger shows his 'communicative intent' and the adult's facial expression confirms, that they are sharing 'joint attention' about me taking a photo.

A child needs to discover language for themselves

In order to be able to discover in himself his own ability to use vocal sounds in order to speak, a child needs to

→ *PLAY WITH MAKING SOUNDS in fun ways (not speech play!) by himself and together with another person*

→ *allow their MOUTH to be liberated from the physical function of infantile eating, so it can be used for experimenting with sounds and vocalizing (i.e. constant sucking, eating, drinking from bottles, sweets, dummies inhibit this process), but also with multi-dimensional chewing (e.g. meat, raw carrots)*

→ *let their MIND generate images, memories, ideas and 'dream-thoughts' and to have time to process these, to think and communicate about what he is feeling about what he is doing, rather then mindless actions and movement*

→ *increase his ability to WAIT and to discover his ability to regulate himself, i.e. to be able to tolerate frustration without falling apart when he doesn't get instant sensory satisfaction*

→ *be interested to make LINKS with their immediate experience and the images, sounds, music, smells, sensations, feelings and emotional atmosphere around him*

→ *find a PERSON who is paying attention to his efforts to find gestures or other non-verbal ways to express his dream-thoughts, ideas and memories*

Mum is joining her child and helping him to succeed with his intention of making the pens 'explode' from the kitchen-roll he had posted them into

Dialogue games

Remember the early baby-games that practice pure communication and dialogue-skills? We do not need words to have a conversation! If we copy his sounds or movements, he is likely to respond with delight and echo them. At that moment we are having a dialogue, a babbling conversation or a movement dialogue!

Understanding language

Understanding language begins with the child feeling like a powerful communicator and the repeated experience of people around him who love and understand what he means when using his body to express what is in his mind.

> **LANGUAGE DEVELOPMENT IS LIKE AN ORCHESTRA**
> Sounds, meanings, words, motivation, thoughts, grammar, rules, joint attention, sharing ideas, making an effort all have to play together harmoniously.

Problems with understanding of language

If your child has problems with understanding language and what you say to him, you need to help him to understand the MEANING of communication first by reducing your language and focusing more on gestural communication, e.g. if he:

→ imitates words without meaning
→ misinterprets what you say and responds in ways that don't make sense
→ does not respond to what is said to him
→ shows confusion and dysregulation

Developmental strategies to help your child to understand language

1. *Look at what the child is looking at*
2. *Use language in context, as the child will try to make sense of what he sees is happening around him*
3. *Use gestural language to help your child to understand, i.e. so he can 'see what he hears'*
4. *Reduce complexity: Keep language simple (but without distorting your grammar), i.e. avoid long sentences,*
5. *Maintain grammar, melody and flow: use correct language, i.e. don't use grammatically incorrect language as this affects its meaning*
6. *Repeat the relevant language or words in meaningful ways (i.e. not to 'teach' or 'test') and many different familiar situations*
7. *Match language with child's actions and feelings: be Playful, firstly engaging in 1-1 sensory and action games (shared attention), later toys (joint attention)*
8. *Do what makes sense and what you usually do with objects, i.e. don't put the cup upside down, until child understands that putting a cup on your head is a playful game*
9. *SLOW DOWN and keep a slow/moderate pace, so your child can follow and has time to process*

In a nutshell

1. *Reduce complexity*
2. *Maintain correct grammar, melody and flow*
3. *Pair language with child's actions*
4. *Link timing and contextual support, so the child can experience action, feelings and words at the same time.*
5. *Present the same words in many familiar settings*

Sound effects come before words and are the first step towards talking, as they match vocal sounds with the child's actions and feelings.

Growing up with more than one Language

'Should I speak English with him at home, although I don't speak good English myself?' – No.

This advice is often given by school, nursery or other staff, who don't speak other languages except English, because of a mistaken idea that it would make life easier, if they can understand the child. But it is bad advice. Research shows that this is the worst you can do, if you want to help your child to learn to talk.

Over 60% of the world grow up with more than one language

Children need to learn to speak one language well and with correct grammar and pronunciation. In order to do so, a child needs fluent and correct language input in their family in the first years at home. In most bilingual or multi-lingual families, this will be the family language or mother tongue.

If parents speak with the child in English or a language, that is not their own and that they aren't fluent in or find difficult to pronounce, then the child cannot learn any language well, neither the family language nor English or other 'environmental' language of school, which is the worst start possible.

The majority of people in the world are multi-lingual

→ More children in the world grow up speaking more than one language.

→ English is very useful. But it is only one of many world-languages, each best suited to describe its particular world.

→ A second or additional language expands our horizon, makes room for imagination and creativity, and helps to be aware of the limitations of our cultural perspectives.

→ Children growing up with more than one language learn to speak in the same way as children growing up with only one language.

The mother tongue of these Bolivians is Aymara, – one of several official languages in Bolivia including Spanish.
Who can speak English with the visitors who don't speak Spanish?

Best conditions for learning more than one language:

→ stable and harmonious living situation at home

→ intensive contact for the child with speakers of both/all languages at the child's level

→ regular travel to the country of the 'other language' to hear it being used in context

→ having fun together when talking in any of the child's languages (i.e. not just 'teaching' lessons)

→ being able to speak the language of the environment well before beginning nursery/school

Language learning follows the same process, whether growing up with one or more languages.

Every Child can Learn

Every child can learn, if our focus is on the child's potential, i.e. on what the child can do rather than on what they cannot do, whatever his challenges, diagnosis or learning difficulties. With well enough informed help, a child who has missed out due to learning difficulties or other challenges can catch up with what he has missed out and continue to learn, whatever his diagnosis or developmental delay. Referring to her 'Developmental Sequence of Basic Activities and Learning' as described in our chapter about babies, Carol Mannion, a Developmental Therapist, says 'the autistic child seems somehow to be stuck in earlier stages of development. If we can identify where the child seems to have got stuck in his development, then we can help him to catch up where he may have missed out.'

The Waldon Approach is about the growth of understanding and the most basic elements of human learning and development. www.waldonassociation.org.uk

Most 'functional learning' materials are simple objects that are easy to collect, make or obtain (illustration from 'Every child can learn', Katrin Stroh et al.)

The 'Functional Learning' Waldon Approach, described and illustrated Katrin Stroh's book 'Every child can learn', Sage 2008, ISBN-10: 1412947952

is a practical intervention approach aiming to 'unlock a child's potential through interactive learning, directed exploration and basic problem solving'. It is a theory about the most basic elements of human learning and development. Children with developmental delay, learning difficulties, autism or other disabilities often do not spontaneously explore and learn from their environment. In fact, one could say that their main problem is that 'they don't understand'. By helping the child through the developmental sequence of simple movement activities with everyday objects we can help them to build the foundation on which language and all further learning can build.

In **'Autism and Understanding. The Waldon Approach to Child Development'** Walter Solomon, the father of Robert, once severely autistic, describes how his son was helped by this approach. Robert is now married with a good job and a lovely baby daughter. The book about his recovery is being published by Sage Publications in 2012. www.autismandunderstanding.com.

'Understanding Understanding': How does Understanding Develop?

Geoffrey Waldon, a neurologist who developed the idea of 'Functional Learning' described two complementary kinds of understanding:

General Understanding, the universal comprehension of the world and how it and our bodies work, is similar in all countries, climates, and cultures throughout history, and is basic to all human beings. General Understanding is not taught but is acquired internally by the child as he plays and explores the environment, i.e. before there are rules or 'right and wrong', and it lays the foundations for language development and imaginative play.

Cultural Understanding comes later, is molded by the specific external requirements of the family and their culture, and varies as much as all the languages in the world. It differs according to country or region, social classes within the area, and every family style and history, including the gender of the child. It is meant to prepare the child to fit into the society in which he is growing up. It is taught to the child by the people around and directing and supporting him as in order to take his place in society a child needs to learn the particular cultural norms of that society. But it cannot develop without a solid foundation in 'general understanding'. http://www.waldonassociation.org.uk/

Two Kinds of Understanding

General Understanding: the foundation of all other learning, cannot be taught, only happens through movement
Particular/Cultural Understanding is taught to help child to conform to the rules of the society in which he lives

General Understanding	Particular Understanding
No right or wrong	→ *About right and wrong*
No rules	→ *Rules must be followed*
No adult teaching	→ *Teaching by adult*
Motivated to experiment	→ *Told what to do and how*
The more effort, the better	→ *The less effort, the better*
Child does it for his own enjoyment	→ *Child does it for adult's approval*

Primary and secondary impediments

Waldon distinguishes between a "primary impediment" which is the intrinsic physical/mental problem affecting development, and 'secondary impediments' which are learned behaviours as a result of the primary problem.

'The Potato Game': Simple placing activity to develop rhythm and hand-eye coordination

Placing and sorting different coloured rings, without help

Sorting and placing activity using containers and coloured bricks

Matching objects with a picture, – first the same, later with picture of similar objects

Avoidance or 'handicapping' behaviours such as having a tantrum, stiffening the body, averting the gaze, indulging in annoying and inappropriate social behaviour
Self-delighting behaviours such as rocking, spinning and head banging

The Asocial Lesson aims to give the child experience in movements/activities to strengthen his general under-standing. The facilitator is behind or to the side of the child and prompts and assists, – without praise.

Girl enjoying her 'asocial lesson': placing cardboard rings onto a long stick using 'big movements'

Early stage understanding will be reinforced by: Banging, Scraping, Placing ... leading to
Precursor stage: Pairing, Separating, Sequencing, Piling and Scribbling ... leading to
Learning-to-Learn-Tools which are Matching, Sorting, Seriation, Brick Building, Drawing and Coding

Waldon Activities

(use real objects first, then simple drawings, then pictures):
Objects are put down one at a time in front of the child, who picks each one up and puts it into the target container

→ **Placing:** *picking things up and putting them down*
→ **Piling:** *by piling things up children discover the properties of objects, e.g. weight, size, texture, how things move and fall if put on top of another*
→ **Banging** *is the basis of a child's ability to grasp, hold and make use of tools, e.g. spoon, drawing*
→ **Pairing:** *bringing together objects that are the same*
→ **Matching:** *learning about similarities and differences, e.g. objects that are similar but not the same*
→ **Sorting:** *recognising that objects can be the same/similar and can be grouped into sets/categories, which requires a firm foundation of placing, pairing and matching*
→ **Sequencing:** *a complex form of thinking that has a linear movement, e.g. events that take place one after another and can be repeated, involving rhythm, e.g. actions songs, dressing, speech*
→ **Brick-building:** *understanding of 3-dimensional complex relationships between different objects and forces, i.e. understanding spatial relationships, – requires firm foundation of placing, piling, matching and sorting*
→ **Scribbling and drawing:** *understanding 2-dimensional space, necessary for understanding symbols*
→ **Coding** *is the process by which one thing can be allowed to stand for another and can only develop when the other learning-to-learn-tools are in place and interconnecting.*

Variations:

different speed, different objects, different positions

Understanding Autistic States of Mind

Some of the underlying processes behind the external features of autism can be described using insights from modern attachment theory and psycho-analytic object-relations theory, particularly Bion and other autism-specialists like F. Tustin, D. Meltzer, A. Alvarez, S. Spensley, P. Hobson, F. Scabbiolo and others.

Autistic children seem to be caught in a time-warp, – unable to use their mind to manage what is going on inside and around them. They use sensation-dominated activities/movement to create a sense of being inside a hard shell to shut out all awareness of difference. Cut off from relationships with people, stranded in a world almost completely dominated by the sense of touch and sensations, the autistic child sometimes seems to feel like something inanimate teetering on the edge of becoming alive and a person. As a result, he is in the grip of horrifying terrors. To avoid these, autistic children sometimes seem to resort to feeling they are floating (hence perhaps on tip-toes), weightlessly high above the ordinary world of human beings, where 'to be or not to be' is not an issue. The reasons for this are always multi-facetted, including very early psychological and physiological processes, including hypersensitivities, sensory integration difficulties and associated relationship issues. Sometimes, these hyper-sensitive babies, in immature state of neuro-mental organisation, may have had a traumatic moment of unbearable awareness of being alone/separate from their feeding mother, got into a panic about their helplessness, – and withdrew. Aspects of autistic states of mind can be described by the following processes:

1. 'Tactile hallucinations': Unconceptualised protective practices:
Autistic sensation objects and shapes could be described as 'tactile hallucinations' that protect against the terrors of 'not-being'. But they obstruct ongoing psychological development, because they re-enforce the autistic child's peculiar reactions to space and relationships.

   a. 'Autistic (Sensation) Objects' make the child feel hard and impenetrable, and give him a sense of security. They are usually hard, and the child feels that the hardness/ sharp edges/ 'twiddliness'/... is part of his own body and will make him safe and impenetrable, e.g. toy-car, train, – initially bodily sensations like hard rolled-up tongue, hard faeces in anus, hard bunches of flesh inside cheeks, e.g. child biting all corners/ hard edges of photos, books, toys

   b. 'Autistic (Sensation) Shapes' are tactile activities to produce whorls of sensations that are felt to wrap the body surfaces in a comforting and soothing way (like tranquilisers) to produce a sense of ongoingness in order to avoid the painful awareness of separateness, e.g. stroking, rubbing, smearing, licking, ...usually on smooth surfaces/skin, – also rocking, fidgeting, flapping, spinning, also running, climbing, ... The experience is in terms of surfaces, and the world of the autistic child can be thought of as flat and 2-dimensional without an awareness of the inside of objects, e.g. obsession with running water

2. Bodily Terrors of Damage dominate much of the autistic child's experience, because of his lack of a secure sense of self and personhood. S/he has no concept of growth and healing, and therefore fears bodily damage, rather than being wounded, e.g. holes to their shell, parts of body coming off, leaking out, or that they can be 'gone', lost or forgotten, e.g. fear of ketchup/ colour red, of washing hands/ hair, of own and others' teeth, clutching hard object, or fears of falling through cracks, floorboards, open stairs, even the space between the cushions on the settee.

3. **Touch and turning away from life and from people:** touch has magical significance for autistic children, whose experience is as if it can make them exist or be 'gone'. But their manipulative touching activities, e.g. lining things up, fiddling, using mother's hand, block the development of abstract processes such as thinking, imagination and symbolic processes.

4. **Autistic obstructions to Symbol Formation**

    a. **Perception:** hearing and seeing, which are 'long-distance modes of perception', don't have normal importance for autistic children, who can appear deaf, or even blind, although there is no physical damage, because their attention is riveted on tactile sensations, instead of making sense of sights/sounds. This interferes with the development of percept and concept formation, needed for language-development, which requires some degree of abstraction, e.g. 'tuning out', looking from corner of the eyes, listening to distant noises, 'far-away-eyes'.

    b. **Concept Formation** occurs when objects become classified/ differentiated from each other. For this to happen they need to be
    1. recognised by their specific shape, which
    2. leads to 'percepts' that acquire names through joint attention with mother/carer, which
    3. leads to concept formation giving rise to the 'language revolution'.
    But autistic children live mainly in the subjective, non-shared terms of clusters of auto-generated sensations derived from tactile sensations, i.e. lack of distance/ close proximity: the tactile nature of something (e.g. soft/hard, sharp/rounded corners) is more important than its objective function, thus obstructing percept and concept formation, e.g. any hard object will do, or only one particular cup will do, flapping anything (ribbon, books, doll by its hair, hand).

    c. **Symbol Formation** is a unique feature of human beings/ the human mind and the basis of language, play and thinking. Symbolic development needs a sense of bodily separateness from the outside world, and an ability to use one's mind to deal with the experience of loss, frustration and need. Autistic objects and shapes prevent the use of one's mind for managing difficult feelings, therefore leaving children alone with explosive feelings of excitement, frustration, boredom, emptiness, fears, obsessions, terrors, rage, tantrums

5. **Dismantling** describes an unconscious process in which someone's mind is stripped of its meaning-giving qualities. This process of letting their mind fall apart and rendering their senses and feelings into unconnected experiences of sensation, that cannot be symbolised or thought about, can be a passive process or a more active deliberate one. A person can be more passively sucked into or overrun by, or more actively seek, resist, use, even play with such meaningless mindlessness, e.g. watching moving patterns of clouds/ tree/ cars with far-away eyes, listening to mother's tone of voice not her words, mindlessly being absorbed in (usually) moving patterns, like TV and video.

Autistic children need a caring person's thoughtful awareness and the digestive reflective functions of another person's mind, trying to understand and make sense of, or give meaning to their behaviours, sensations and experiences, and to draw them into emotionally reciprocal human relationships that will provide the child with an alternative way of managing difficult feelings and experiences. It is the emotionality in the contact which promotes change in social relatedness, communication and thoughtfulness.

Engaging Autism through Play

MindBuilders' approach as described in this book is greatly influenced by the DIR-Floortime approach as developed by Dr. S. Greenspan and S. Wieder, PhD. This positive, dynamic and playful approach redefines autism as a developmental disorder with great potential for growth and change. It makes sense of its puzzling symptoms with the help of their universal model of mental-emotional development. Sometimes children need extra help to grow these mental-emotional skills without which other cognitive, social, emotional, language, and motor skills as well as their sense of self cannot reach its full developmental potential. You will find a lot more useful information on www.floortime.org

Understanding the 'Functional Emotional Developmental Levels' that build the mind provides us with a direction for successful intervention. Its aims are not so much 'autism-specific' but the same as every parent would have for their child: increasing emotional engagement, warm relationships with others, communicating with gestures and talking meaningfully, and it maps out strategies, techniques and activities to achieve this.

What is DIR-Floortime?

Floortime (www.floortime.org) is a child-centred approach that focuses on building relationships through interaction and play. Floortime is a specific technique to both follow the child's natural emotional interests (lead) and at the same time challenge the child towards increasing mastery of his social, emotional and intellectual capacities. This means that the adult joins the child in what they are doing, rather than trying to teach the child what the adult wants them to do. In Floortime, adult and child aim to have fun together through playful interactions on the 'floor' (hence the name 'Floortime'), or later through conversations and interactions in other places.

Sometimes children need extra help to grow these mental-emotional skills without which other cognitive, social, emotional, language, and motor skills as well as their sense of self cannot reach its full developmental potential.

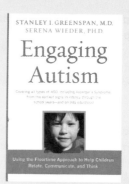

Engaging autism: Using the Floortime Approach to Help Children Relate, Communicate, and Think by Stanley I. Greenspan, M.D. and Serena Wieder, PhD, ISBN 0738210943

In Floortime, the adult follows the child's lead or woos him into emotional engagement, with the aim to have fun together through playful interaction

Sound effects come before words and are the first step towards talking, as they match vocal sounds with the child's actions and feelings

DIR = Developmental – Individual-Difference – Relationship-Based

The objectives of the DIR®/Floortime™ Model are to build healthy foundations for social, emotional and intellectual capacities rather than focusing on skills or learning specific behaviours.

Developmental – There are 6 basic functional developmental levels that form the foundation for all of a child's relationships and learning, with each level building on the next like a developmental ladder. (See Functional Emotional Developmental Levels, FEDLs, next page)

Individual differences – each child is different with their own unique biologically-based ways of responding to and relating to the world, which needs our careful attention.

Relationship-based – a child's mind needs warm relationships with people who care and who tailor their interactions sensitively to the child's individual differences and developmental capacities to enable progress in mastering the essential foundations

Developmental foundations of relationships and learning

The child need to be able to

→ *attend and remain calm and regulated,*
→ *engage and relate to others,*
→ *initiate and respond to all types of communication beginning with emotional and social affect based gestures,*
→ *engage in shared social problem-solving and intentional behavior involving a continuous flow of interactions in a row,*
→ *use ideas to communicate needs and think and play creatively,*
→ *build bridges between ideas in logical ways which lead to higher level capacities to think in multi-causal, grey area and reflective ways.*

This boy is easier to engage in interactive games, when he is lying down and his body is supported.

Individual sensory differences, such as being overly sensitive to sound, affect how a child relates to the world.

Many children with an autism diagnosis have difficulties with self-regulation and seek out excitement through jumping and other thrill-seeking behaviours.

Functional Emotional Developmental Levels (FEDL):
Adapted from Dr. Solomon's PLAY-Project™ Materials ©

Level 1: Self-Regulation, Shared Attention + Interest in the World (about 0-3 months).
The child's ability to enter and sustain a state of shared attention with another person and stay focused, organized and calm.
Adult does 100% of initiation to sustain shared attention, doing almost all of the work to get attention/ looks and modulating the pace of play for regulation.

Level 2: Engagement and Relating (about 2 to 7 months)
The ability to form relationships/ attachment and to engage another person with warmth and pleasure.
Adult still does most of the initiation to 'woo' child into engaging, 'entertaining' child to get laughter, smiles, affect.
Child will sustain engagement in reciprocal interactions.

Level 3: Two-Way Intentional Communication (about 3-10 months).
Back and forth affective signaling and communication to convey intentions, interests and needs.
Child begins to initiate purposeful back and forth interactions (ping-pong) around desires (opening circles) and will close circles following adult's response to his initiative and begins to have his own ideas.
Adult does more waiting for child's intent and feels some sharing of the work for the first time.

Level 4: Purposeful Problem-Solving Communication (about 9 to 18 months).
The ability to use complex circles of communication by stringing together a series of gestures, actions and words into an elaborate problem solving sequence of interactions which helps child develop a sense of self.
Child is now responsible for half of the relationship through initiating 50% with
Adult waiting more/for problem-solving.

Level 5: Creating and Elaborating Ideas (Symbols) (about 24 to 30 months).
The child's ability to create ideas (symbols) observed in pretend play and words (phrases and sentences) to convey some emotional intention
Child can engage in long conversations to communicate interests, feelings, desires and objections ... using ideas/words to convey feelings and intentions.
Adult works at expanding child's pretend play and by asking 'wh'-questions

Level 6: Building Bridges between Ideas (Logical Thinking) (about 36-48 months).
The ability to build logical bridges or make connections between different emotional ideas (emotional thinking).
Child is challenged to connect his ideas by seeking his opinion, enjoying his debates and negotiate what he wants using logical reasons.
Adult works with child keeping him 'on his toes', challenging child to think as well as opening to other's perspectives.

DIR-Floortime Principles

→ **Circles of communication/interaction** are the back and forth of **non-verbal 'ping-pong'** or turn-taking that is the basis of all conversation, and we want the child to take his part in the dialogue as much as possible, – which means that **YOU must leave GAPS for HIM to take HIS turn**. Our most important aim is to help the child to increase the number and complexity of circles of communication and for him to initiate and sustain the dialogue himself.

→ **Language development** is essentially an emotional issue. Language is above all a carrier of emotional communication and meaning, and so much more than just speech or words or names of objects. Words can be learnt easily once emotional communication between child and family provides a secure base for the child to pick up the emotional meanings of what is said through non-verbal communication, the 'music of language', tones of voice, gestures, playfulness, facial expressions, etc.

→ **The emotional drives the cognitive**, not the other way round, i.e. children learn best when they are motivated, and we are all motivated by things we love and enjoy and that make us feel that we can succeed and do well.

→ **Relationships and attachment are the basis of all learning and healthy development,** i.e. the important thing is to engage emotionally with the child as the unique person he is, and not, like in some teaching-approaches, as an animal to be trained/drilled or a computer to be programmed.

→ **'Meet them where they're at … and take them where they need to go' (Greenspan)**, i.e. meet your child at his current level and build on his strengths to help him develop his weaker sides better.

→ **Follow your child's lead** = 'tune into his interests and desires in interactions and play to harness the power of his motivation and help him climb the developmental ladder' (www.floortime.org)

→ **Pay attention to your child's attention**, i.e. join your child's interests and what he is doing and what he WANTS to do through playful interactions, i.e. engage and 'woo' the child, – rather than imposing or 'teaching', which can be annoying, – except when the child is asking for teaching

→ **Enter your child's world** to help him to relate meaningfully in spontaneous and flexible ways, and help to **Extend and expand on your child's ideas**

→ **Don't do for him, what he can do for himself:** having 'a problem' is not bad, but a healthy challenge for thinking, communicating and mental-emotional growth

→ **PLAY-Cues** are the critical unit of observation. They are the behaviors that tell you, what the child wants to do. They may be verbal, but most often they are non-verbal. A cue tells you whether the child is enjoying, tolerating or not enjoying the interaction. By being sensitive and attentive to cues, you discover the child's intent. Cues guide interaction and circles of communication to keep you contingent ('cued' in) and in 'The Dance of Relationship'. Cues can be obvious or very subtle; positive or negative, e.g. Frowning (-), Moving away (-), Smiling (+), Giving eye contact (+), Stiffening, Permitting, Pausing …

→ **SLOW DOWN and TUNE IN** to feel your child's rhythm, so you can share it. LISTEN to his breathing. WATCH and follow his shifting attention. Tune in and respond to his faint cues.

Play and Language for Autistic Youngsters*

The PLAY-Project (Play and Language for Autistic Youngsters) is a practical application of the DIR-Floortime model created by Dr. Rick Solomon, a behavioural-developmental pediatrician with many years of experience of working directly with children and families living with ASD. Look out for his forthcoming book 'Autism: The Potential Within', which is telling the story of how the PLAY-Project helped the parents or a boy with autism to climb up the developmental ladder towards language, play and meaningful relationships. See: www.playproject.org

Dr. Rick Solomon (USA) during his first visit to the UK discussing how to implement the PLAY-Project in Tower Hamlets/London with Khalida Khan, Dr. Nawal Albustani and Sibylle Janert

→ A parent training model devised by Dr. Rick Solomon to teach parents techniques that are effective, fun and useful in day-to-day interactions.
→ as an innovative solution to the lack of effective services for young children with autism and their families in the light of massively rising numbers of children diagnosed with autism/ASD
→ as a practical application of the DIR-Floortime model of the respected child psychiatrist, Dr. Stanley Greenspan and Serena Wieder, www.floortime.org
→ incorporating all of the 6 factors for positive outcomes to reduce the severity of a child's autism as identified by Ramey and Ramey (1998).

Family-centred PLAY-home consultation coaching dad and sister in effective play and Floortime strategies

How to reduce the severity of a child's autism?
6 Factors for positive outcomes (Ramey and Ramey 1998):
1. the earlier the better
2. long-term (usually 2-3 years) and intensive, i.e. between 15-25 hours/week
3. work directly with the child, about 2 hours/day, rather than parent-training only (as in EarlyBird),
4. involving and coaching parents as the prime agents for change,
5. recognition of each child's individual differences,
6. to take place as much as possible at home.

Coaching mum on how to attend to her child's intention in order to re-engage

For best progress the child must have sufficient time (at least 1-2 years) for PARENTS to work AT HOME with their child and PLAY-Home Consultant BEFORE the child begins to attend groups/nursery. In order to be ready for school/groups a child needs to be at least at FEDL 3/4.

The autistic child's refusal to engage in social play can be confusing and intimidating.

Parents are the most important 'agents for change' Why parents?

... Because parents are the real experts on their child

→ Parents spend more time with their children than all of their teachers and therapists combined.

→ By training parents to be their child's best P.L.A.Y. partner, the child can receive intensive high quality intervention every day.

→ We recommend that parents/ caregivers, once trained by our Home Consultant, then spend at least 2 hours every day PLAYing with their child, usually in shorter (e.g. 6x20-minute) sessions, which can/will be a very enjoyable time for you with your child.

→ This type of PLAY assists the child to work through the core deficits of autism.

→ This Early Intervention Programme aims to address developmental problems, that a child needs to have mastered BEFORE starting at play-group, nursery or other group-settings

→ and in order to get ready to cope and become ready to learn at school with his peers.

→ Our Home Consultants are experts on autism and have been intensively trained to guide you and to teach you PLAY-techniques, so that you can more effectively assist your child to move up the developmental ladder, and increase language and social skills.

→ Our goal is for you, the parent, to be your child's best P.L.A.Y.-Partner!

But if we don't help and encourage him, when he is young, his difficulties may become more entrenched, confused and increasingly difficult to change.

Recommendations for the education of young children with autism

(US National Institute for Mental Health/NIMH):
Parents and professionals should

→ Begin interventions early (18 months to 5 years)
→ Use intensive intervention 25 hours per week
→ Have an adult/play partner to child ratio of 1:1 or 1:2
→ Use interventions that are engaging and
→ Have a strategic direction, e.g. social skills, language, etc

By joining him in his interests and tuning in to his level, we can help a child to make progress with engaging and being interested in loving interactions: the earlier, the better!

The Comfort Zone Model*

Comfort zone activities are repetitive asymbolic movements or behaviours that a child does when they are left to do anything they want:

→ Repetitive, restrictive behaviours make it seem as if child doesn't want to be part of our world.

→ These perseverative/stereotypical 'autistic' behaviours are not 'bad'.

→ They are a form of comfort the child uses to make himself feel safe and regulated in what feels to him like an anxiety-provoking world.

→ They may become habits & keep the child isolated.

→ 'Joining' these 'autistic behaviours' helps engagement (FDL2).

→ As the child's world view enlarges, these 'autistic behaviours' will diminish naturally.

Some children with autism are fascinated by spinning objects like wheels, fans, washing machines ...

Comfort zone activities are not 'bad' and a child should be allowed to withdraw to his comfort zone at times in order to calm down, when s/he has felt overwhelmed by a sense of 'too-much-ness', which can be due to strong emotions, over-stimulation, or boredom and not knowing what to do next. But we then want to join him there and gently WOO him out and back into human relationships and engaging with another person emotionally.

A child's comfort zone activities will get less as he moves up the developmental ladder and becomes more emotionally engaged and able to communicate with other people.

If we try to stop a child in their comfort zone activities, these will in fact increase, because he will become more anxious and therefore more insistent on tuning out and withdrawing into his comfort zone away from human interaction and emotional communication.

'Funny looking': one of this boy's comfort zone activities is focusing his eyes to squint at the line of cars

Some Comfort zone activities:

→ Lining up blocks, trains, cars, trucks, dolls

→ Turning lights/water on and off

→ Water play/flushing toilets/watching water

→ Watching blinds/edges/ spinning things

→ Licking, mouthing, smelling

→ Watching the same videos over and over

→ Playing with mobile phones, on computer

→ Holding objects in his/her hands, esp. Thomas train

→ Humming/making noises

→ Flapping hands/a ribbon

Eye-games: Playing with his vision, rather than using his eyes for looking and seeing

The Comfort Zone model can be used to plan **play sequences** to engage your child.

1. Start **engagement** with physical **sensory motor play**, i.e. through touch, rhythm or movements.
2. Turn the play into **games** that have a clear 'beginning – middle – end', so you can repeat them and your child knows 'what comes next' and what to expect in the predictable sequence of the game
3. Add simple words/ sound effects and **'highlight your language'**, e.g. 'IN! ... and ...OUT!', 'UP and DOWN', 'ready – steady – go!' so your child can pick out the important words easily
4. Eventually introduce **imagination**, i.e. encouraging your child to use his mind more for thinking and problem-solving. Avoid too much excitement as this makes thinking and using the mind more difficult.
5. By following this sequence, you help your child to establish **simple relationships** (FDL 1-4)
6. Leading to more **complex relationships** including language, thinking and story-telling (FDL 5 & 6)

Comfort Zone Behaviour: Returning to a foetal position of pre-natal safety.

PLAY- Techniques*

Dr. Solomon's PLAY Techniques are graded according to functional developmental levels so as to help parents and professionals

→ to be more resourceful and to feel less helpless with their child's autistic behaviours
→ to expand the child's alertness and awareness
→ to improve the child's capacity to take the initiative and become more flexible
→ to increase the numbers and complexity of 'circles of communication'
→ to encourage the child's ability to solve problems
→ to play more joyfully by 'going for AFFECT' (feelings), so that all can have FUN together!

Joining: This boy likes to push his train around the room. His mother 'joins' him using her slipper.

Mirroring: by following his lead, the child's solitary play becomes a shared experience, – and he loves it!

PLAY-Techniques FDL 1-4*

Attention/Engagement and Two Way Communication:

1. Being With/Go for Affect
2. Sensory-motor Play
3. Theme & Variation
4. Taffy Pulling
5. Salient Language
6. Rhythm & Music
7. Sense of Humor, Suspense, Surprise
8. One and Two Step Commands
9. Playful obstruction
10. Making them work
11. Rewarding/Reinforcing
12. Making behaviors purposeful
13. Expectant waiting
14. Going for fun
15. Big, little, & micro circles
16. Add a word
17. Asked and answered
18. Sequences/little stories
19. Problem solving

Expectant waiting

→ Waiting is a primary technique but it must be **expectant** waiting i.e. waiting for a return response. This can be a look, a (tiny) gesture, or even just waiting expectantly in return from him. However, you DO want to get him to understand that you DO expect him to make some sound or other clear communication, and not just to wait passively for YOU to do the 'work'.

→ Expectant waiting helps children to initiate (= the essence of Greenspan Functional Level 3).

→ The key here is to **make an overture**, – and **then WAIT** to see what the child wants to do.

→ If he does not respond, – then perhaps you do something a little different which he did not expect, – so that for you to do what he DID want you to do, he would have to tell you somehow ...

→ **Waiting** allows you to **observe** the child more accurately and to increase circles of interaction

PLAY-Techniques FDL 4-6*
Shared Meanings & Emotional Thinking

1. Simple pretend play
2. More complex pretend play
3. Multiple circles of communication
4. Feelings, Empathy
5. Outings
6. Using motivation
7. Appropriate Language
8. Essays
9. Answering 'wh' questions
10. Time Concepts
11. Practicing Pronouns
12. Model, Rehearse, Expect
13. Theory of Mind: Puppet Play
14. Social Stories
15. Meta-cognitive strategies

To buy a pack of PLAY-cards FDL 1-2 or FDL 4-6 @ £10 +p/p per pack www.mindbuilders-consulting.org

Speaking TO and Speaking FOR the Child.

→ Speaking to the child is easy. It means not baby talking, but using appropriate language.

→ Talk to the child in normal tones, rhythms and usage. Let them hear the music of the language.

→ Speaking 'for' the child is trickier. It involves modeling language for the child from the child's perspective i.e. **'What would the child say if he could say what he means?'**

→ = You speak 'for' him.

→ For example, the child says, 'Ice-cream!' You say, 'I want ice-cream, mummy.' as if YOU were the child.

→ Or the child says 'No no!' and you say, 'No, don't do that. I don't like that, daddy!.'

PLAY-Activities by Developmental Levels*

Here some suggestions of activities to play with your child at the different Functional Developmental Levels. Some of these you will find illustrated with more details to stimulate your imagination in 'PLAYing and Autism'.

FEDL 1-2: PLAY-Activities: 'Fishing' for engagement*

At this level the adult's task is to keep in mind:

1. **How can I ENGAGE my child?**
2. **How can I MAKE his/her solitary activities INTERACTIVE and FUN?**

Sensory-Motor Activities:

→ Gently shaking arms or legs
→ Gently squeezing arms, leg, head, ...
→ Gently pound rhythms on his back
→ Swinging child in a blanket
→ Pulling child across the floor on a rug/blanket
→ Jumping on the bed, mattress or trampoline
→ Big gym ball
→ Big box for child to sit in: move it, rock it, turn it, shake it ... to a rhythm or song
→ Tickling and gentle wrestling (keep tickling to a minimum)
→ Blowing on their skin, hair, face
→ Action-rhymes and songs
→ Turning the lights on and off
→ Flicking pages of a book
→ Opening and closing a door and playing peek a boo from the other side
→ Rolling child up in a rug
→ Gently lying/sitting on child to give them a sensation of pressure
→ Spinning child on a swivel chair: stop saying 'Stop!', then spin it saying 'Go!'
→ Building blocks up and knocking them down, saying 'Up – up – up' as you build and 'Crash!' as you knock them
→ Dropping things and making a noise as they fall: 'boom!'
→ Sensory 'Feely box': fill a shallow plastic box (about the size of an A4 paper) with sensory material, e.g. lentils, different colour beans, cornflour and water, brillo pads, marbles, etc. for sensory exploration
→ Shaving foam on a table
→ Water play of all kinds (bath, sink, water-bowl, hose, with bubbles, etc.)

> **MAIN TECHNIQUES TO USE AT FEDL 1-2:**
> 1. **RHYTHM, REPETITION** and predictable **SEQUENCES**
> 2. **SURPRISE** and **SUSPENSE**
> 3. **NAME** and talk to his **GESTURES** and don't expect speech

Swinging a child in a blanket is a great sensory activity, that can be made interactive.

FDL 3-4: PLAY-Activities: 'Going for Circles'*

At this level the adult's task is to keep in mind how to encourage the child to:

1. **INITIATE and to open and close multiple circles?**
2. **KEEP CIRCLES GOING and to stay engaged for longer and longer**
3. **PROBLEM SOLVE with the help of other people?**

> **MAIN TECHNIQUES TO USE AT FEDL 2-4:**
> 1. Don't do too much, but
> 2. **WAIT EXPECTANTLY** for child to initiate
> 3. Give him problems to solve.
> 4. Don't do for him, what he can do for himself.

→ Chase: 'I'm gonna get you'
→ Get the bubbles, balloon, etc.
→ Being silly, playing slap-stick
→ Ready-steady-go games
→ Ball play: rolling/throwing/tossing/handing it back and forth
→ Skittles and ball (plastic bottles work fine)
→ Getting in the way games: 'It's stuck. Can you open it?'
→ Obstacle course, e.g. onto chair – jump off – under table – clap-clap-clap! + repeat
→ Finger painting with shaving cream, colored glue with sparkles, etc.
→ Peek a boo games: hide under covers, peek around the corner, ...
→ Very simple pretend play: phone to ear, cars crash+make crashing sound, feed dolly, drink pretend-tea,
→ Making choices about which activities they want to play.
→ 'Blow table tennis': blow small paper/cotton wool, playdough ball, pencil ... to each other across the table
→ Puzzles, Lego, bricks, construction toys, ...
→ Picture matching games, picture lotto, ...
→ Farm animal play, dump trucks, trains
→ Threading big beads
→ Sorting activities: colours, shapes, sizes, categories (cars, busses, trains; animals; spoons, forks; socks, shoes; ...)
→ Action rhymes and songs: Wheels on the bus, Incy wincy spider, ...
→ Horsey-back rides: horsey needs to eat/drink, sleep, rest, ...
→ Like-a-bike (without pedals), scooter board, scooter
→ Big cardboard boxes to sit in, to make house, car, boat, bus, fort, ...
→ Remember to FOLLOW THEIR LEAD!
→ Don't forget to MAKE it so that you have FUN together!

Putting all the family's shoes in ... and out ... and in again involves lots of interaction, simple language and helps with understanding the world around us

FDL 5-6: PLAY-Activities: Shared Meanings and Symbolic Play*

At this level the adult's task is to keep in mind how to encourage the child to:

1. **to encourage THINKING and generating new ideas**
2. **understanding ABSTRACT CONCEPTS, including rules**
3. **managing a wider repertoire of EMOTIONS**

MAIN TECHNIQUES TO USE AT FEDL 5-6:
1. More complex symbolic play
2. Answering wh-questions
3. Helping child to think and reason

→ Pretend: dress up, crashing cars, tea party, dolly sleeping, dinosaurs chasing another, ...
→ Real hide and seek, not just peek-a-a boo. Hide a doll and say 'Where is the dolly?'
→ Picture-books, looking at pictures and telling a simple story (Don't READ the book, but explain what's happening.)
→ Treasure hunt games
→ Obstacle courses
→ Drawing: cars, animals, people, situations (NOT guiding or around child's hand!)
→ Sequencing: cards, pictures, objects
→ Baking and making cakes, helping with cooking
→ Putting things in like groups/categories, planning out schedules
→ Board games – candy land, chutes and ladders, barnyard bingo, memory, go fish,
→ Complex pretend play (making up stories about animals, dolls, etc.)
→ Hide and Seek (with all the rules)
→ Magnetic fishing
→ Group games: Duck, duck, goose; Musical Chairs; Tag; Simon says; Hot Potato
→ Drawing faces with emotions
→ Football, Baseball, T-ball, Dodge ball
→ Jokes
→ Questions and opinions

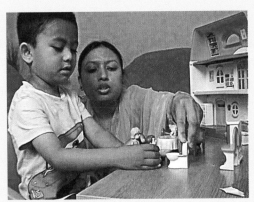

Pretend play with little people: mum helping boy to use the toilet.

* All adapted from Dr. Solomon's PLAY-Project™ materials

Playing and Autism

What is a 'Game'?

But don't just tickle or entertain the child, and don't just 'give him a free ride'! Instead make sure you link your sensory play with structures that helps your child to use his mind for thinking and communicating.

Using the comfort-zone model to organise your **play sequences**, remember to

→ give a **STRUCTURE** and PLAN your play sequences to engage your child by

→ making your **SENSORY-MOTOR PLAY** (touch, rhythm or movements) into

→ **GAMES** that have a clear 'BEGINNING – MIDDLE – END', so you can repeat them and your child knows 'how it works' because he comes to expect a predictable sequence and

→ **ADD SIMPLE SOUND EFFECTS/WORDS** and 'highlight your language', e.g. 'IN! ... and ...OUT!', 'UP and DOWN', 'ready – steady – go!' so your child can pick out the important words easily.

→ Give it a **RHYTHM** and keep it predictable, so it is easy to repeat, i.e. don't keep changing it!

→ **ADD** new small elements once the original structure is really well oiled and practiced

→ Eventually introduce **IMAGINATION** and encourage your child to use his mind more for thinking and problem-solving.

→ Make it **FUN**, but avoid too much excitement as this makes thinking and using the mind more difficult.

Playing for FREE: People Games

Playing with your child does not have to cost money. In fact, many expensive toys have very little play-value (especially battery-toys with buttons to press!). There can be no better toy for your child than another person, who wants to pay attention, interact and play.

> The best interactive toy for your child is YOU!

Using pencils for an interactive game of coordinating shared attention, 'expectant waiting' and 'suspense and surprise', – then 'All fall down!'. And again ...

These are the most basic games that need no toys or any other equipment, just you and the child! But this is also the most effective and can be the most rewarding social activities to help a child with communication difficulties find new joy in relating to another person.

'Make it bigger!' or 'Walking the tightrope between Fear and Delight'

There are two guiding 'principles' to keep in mind that help a child to focus and share attention. One I call **'walking the tightrope between fear and delight'**, using suspense and surprise to keep the child engaged and wondering what is going to happen or what you are going to do next or how or in what slightly different way. It also helps to **'make it bigger'**, i.e. being more dramatic, more emotionally engaging, using more expansive movements, more 'stretch' in your suspense, exaggerating how we speak, its speed, its pitch, its tones. Sometimes this means moving exaggeratedly more slowly, or stopping suddenly, or whispering. We need to make our presence unavoidable for him, but in such fun ways as not to put him off, should he risk coming out of his shell. However, 'making it bigger' does not simply mean more, harder, louder, faster, but **tuning in** sensitively to the child's feeling-state and making it into a shared experience.

'Make it bigger': Trying to attract the child's attention through exaggerating my facial expressions

The success of these games hinges on the adult's under-standing that they are not educational in a functional sense, but about playing with intentions and feelings, about building up expectations, and then stretching, breaking, re-making and mucking about with them, always 'walking the tightrope between fear and delight'.

Looming games are a good way to start engaging the passive child or those who like to lie on their back.

Perhaps the child actually feels somehow a little threat-ened. But there is something odd about this so-called 'threat': it is coming at him and disappearing, or changing, too fast for what would instinctively qualify as a serious threat. The mo-ment he is ready to retreat or run away, the threat itself has retreated. What is going on here? Where has it gone? The child cannot withdraw safely, because that threat is still hanging around somewhere. So he's got to look. The repeated sudden disappearance of the 'threat' coming at him draws his atten-tion to it, his curiosity is engaged, his mind alerted, his senses drawn together into one focus, so unusual for the autistic child, – and so good for him.

If the adult manages to create a situation that is ambigu-ous enough to arouse the need for curiosity, carefully scaf-folded in an atmosphere of friendly affection, then the young autistic child is usually drawn to engage and interact socially in similarly unexpected ways. Some responsive non-autistic capacities may have been hibernating, waiting to be claimed and re-claimed through moments of playful communicative contact, to thrill and enliven the passive or withdrawn child, and the despairing or worn out adult too.

(Janert (2000), Reaching the Young Autistic Child)

Mirroring and Dialogue Games

Focus on the early baby-games that practice pure communication and dialogue-skills. We do not need words to have a conversation! If we copy his sounds, actions or movements, he is likely to respond with delight and echo them. At that moment we are having a dialogue, a babbling conversation or a movement dialogue!

Peekaboo Games

Peekaboo games come naturally with a child with early communication skills and there are so many different ways to play them, – even with your child's feet! Keep it going for as long as possible, and a bit longer than that, and make sure to leave plenty of space for the child to open or close circles, to pull away your hand or to pop up when you didn't expect it … which means that you must WAIT expectantly and for much longer than you often think for HIM to surprise you.

Mirroring the child's intention: it does not have to be the same object for the child to feel understood

Peekaboo games are also very important developmentally as they play with the child's feelings about loss and disappearance and finding again what you thought was lost, with issues around separation and reunion and they help with remembering, motivation and social communication skills.

Looming and 'I'm gonna getcha!' Games

'Im gonna getcha!' games are a version of the Looming games that are familiar to us from our play with babies, in which the adult suddenly and playfully moves forward and into the child's field of vision, saying something like a high-pitched 'hello hello helloooo!' before reeling back again. Looming games are good games to get shared attention and engagement with the child who is more passive or likes to lie on his back, perhaps because of sensory-processing difficulties. With the child who can walk, they become the chasing games of 'I'm going to get you!'-games that every small child loves. Some children love to be caught in your arms, others don't. They may include a small touch or tickle at the end (but keep the tickling to a minimum).

Peekaboo games can played in so many ways. Try to keep it going. And WAIT for the child to initiate!

Mouth and Face Games

Mouth and face games, which really are a larger-than-life version of the baby face-to-face-games of 'pure interaction', are probably the most important 'games' to help an autistic child towards speech and being interested in human interaction. They play on every child's instinctive fascination with mouths, eyes and the emotional expressiveness of faces. Mouths and eyes can open and shut. Mouths have a tongue that moves and is soft and teeth that are hard and solid. Mouths can also make noises and sounds. Eyes can shine and make you feel wonderful, or go dark and make you feel frightened.

Chasing and 'I'm gonna getcha!' games are among the first interactive games

The human FACE is better equipped for this than anything in the world and it is really the most amazing cause-and-effect toy ever invented:

→ *with eyes and a responsive voice,*
→ *guided by a thoughtful and feelingful mind,*
→ *an interest in careful observation,*
→ *sensitive awareness of our own pre-verbal communicative potential,*
→ *a willingness to wait, watch and respond rather than to teach and demand, and*
→ *to keep our concentration tightly focussed on the child's face and subtle communications*

The human face is the most amazing cause-and-effect toy ever invented.

To make these communication games successful, the adult needs to create a sense of anticipation and suspense, often achieved by doing nothing: just waiting, our attention expectantly focussed on the child, like stretching and stretching an imaginary elastic (usually about 10 times longer than you thought you could), increases suspense naturally. An expectant atmosphere in which nothing is happening can be made to produce a grating sense that 'something must be up!', which means that he will have to look at our face to find out: and with that we have eye-contact, interest and engagement!

Mouth and face games allow the child to pay attention to the mouth and the sounds and movements it can make

Example of mouth and face games

'Patrick (age 4 ½) adopted 'Mouth and face-games' as if he had been craving for a game like this:

Always active, it took some time to get Patrick to sit down. To catch his attention I made the most peculiar noise-sequence I could think of with my mouth. He looked up with sudden interest, or suspicion. I did it again, my mind expectantly focussed on him, but paused mid-way waiting for him to complete the sound-sequence. When he did not, I completed it myself more quietly rather than let our hard-won 'joint attention' go. But then he seemed to try, blowing and pressing his lips together, and I echoed him. He did it again, more confidently, and we traded 'raspberries' a few times. I added a tongue-click, and waited for him to try. He did. We now had a 'dialogue-game': 'raspberries – tongue-click – : your turn!'. I added a tongue-wiggle, which he copied. .... And then it was my turn to be surprised. Patrick's response was: 'raspberries' – tongue-click – vocal sound – punch air and shout!' He looked at me with a broad grin, and I copied his expanded version. After 10 minutes he still did not want to stop.'

(Janert (2000), Reaching the Young Autistic Child)

Who is copying whom here?

Mouth and Face Games

Try to get as many circles of communication playing mouth and face games together, making little sequences that you add new elements to, and keep inventing new noises you could make.

→ *Pay attention to your tone of voice: you can make it go UP and DOWN, go SLOW and FAST, suddenly slow down or speed up, ...*

→ *Use your own body-language and tone of voice like a cat to 'CREEP up on him and suddenly POUNCE' and surprise him, in a fun way, when he wasn't expecting it.*

The rhythm and repetition of simple rhymes helps with attention and 'knowing where the words/gestures go'

→ *Make such funny noises with your mouth or tongue that he HAS to look.*

→ *Do it behind him, so he has to turn around.*

→ *Wiggle your tongue, e.g. up and down, side to side, inside your mouth, ... Invent 5 other ways.*

→ *Blow raspberries, plop your lips, ...*

→ *Blow out your cheeks ... blow out ONE cheek only and let him pop it ... then the other*

→ *Bare your teeth ... or clatter your teeth 3x, then stop and wait for him to copy ...*

→ *Pretend to want to bite her fingers ... or nose ... or ear ... or toes ...*

Rhythm and repetition are your best friends in wooing the child into simple interactive games

Music, Rhythm and Musical Games

Music affects us emotionally: it can calm us down and soothe, wake us up, invigorate, energise, ... or annoy, irritate or wind us up. Music is part of human communication, although already animals engage in banging or drumming activities. But only human beings can dance, sing or hum a tune or melody, can drum rhythms that can be repeated in order to express and share their feelings. When we talk, a big part of our communication is in the rhythm and musicality of our tone of voice. In fact, more than twice as much is communicated through our tone of voice than through the words we use to say what we mean. So, make sure you focus on what you communicate with your tone of voice, not just your words, – especially when talking in simple way to a child with low levels of comprehension!

Action songs that involve holding hands help the autistic child to understand and be able to participate

Rhythm and tunes aid recall and help a child to tune in and learn to listen. Listening is a skill that does not necessarily come naturally as it requires the ability to focus on specific sounds and tune out the irrelevant 'noise'. Listening to singing and songs sharpens auditory discrimination, sequencing skills and memory while also encouraging vocal and rhythmic skills, which are part of the basic equipment for learning and language. Songs and rhymes have a simple story line and therefore lay the foundations for the beginnings of story telling.

A basic dialogue consists of a to-and-fro and give-and-take of 'your turn – my turn' as in echoing each other's rhythms, whether in vocal sounds, drumming, humming, clapping, stamping ... Activities such as these lay the foundations for the development of communication and language.

Simple musical activities:
→ *Audio-tapes/CDs of soothing music, e.g. nursery rhymes, classical music (Mozart, Haydn, ...)*
→ *AVOID visual DVDs or screens: they hold the imagination captive instead of leaving the mind free to feel and move*
→ *Dancing to music*
→ *Drumming on drums, cardboard boxes, biscuit tins, tambourine, xylophone ... try to have one each*
→ *Musical cushions: when the music stops, everyone sit down on the nearest cushion on the floor*
→ *Musical freeze: when the music stops, everyone 'freeze'*

Drumming is good for rhythm and interactive games. This boy got his drum to 'Wake up, mummy!', when she pretended to be asleep. She was so surprised!

Drumming:
1. *copy child's rhythms,*
2. *repeat same rhythm and see how long you can keep it going*
3. *expand simple rhythms*
4. *take your time, don't rush it*
5. *trade each other's rhythms*
fast, slow, getting slower, faster, ...

Action-Songs and Rhymes

Nursery rhymes and action-songs are ideal ways to engage an ASD-child, or in fact any child, in shared attention and to help with sensory regulation, initiating communication and imitating actions, and a wonderful way to learn language, rhythm and social skills. Every culture has their own traditional rhymes and songs, but unfortunately a lot of people have now forgotten their tunes, words and actions. MindBuilders' therefore made 2 sets of such rhymes:

MindBuilders' Rhyme Cards by Sibylle Janert and Carol Mannion

Card Set 1
Interactive Rhymes (FDL1-2)
for having Fun with a Child who is Difficult to Engage, ISBN 978-0-9557866-2-4

Card Set 2
Cooperative Rhymes (FDL3/4)
to Woo a Child into Interaction and Shared Play, ISBN 978-0-9557866-3-1

To buy a set of Rhyme cards @ £10 +p/p contact www.mindbuilders-consulting.org

Recommended nursery rhyme Audio CDs:
Genevieve Jereb: Cool bananas, Say G'day, ...
Hap Palmer: What a miracle, Peekaboo, ...
Sherry Shellenberger and Mary Sue Williams: No worries. Songs for sensory modulation.

Movement and Sensory-Motor Activities

Sensory-motor play, movement games or body-gymnastics are often the way in to reach and engage children who spend a lot of time in their comfort zone. Movement integrates the nervous system and is therefore extremely regulating and organising. Sensitive sensory stimulation from an attentive adult can 'wake them up' and get them more interested in the world around them. However, we must be careful not to let it turn into mechanical movement of just going through the motions. Make sure you keep the play alive, soulful, interactive and emotionally engaging. Have fun TOGETHER!

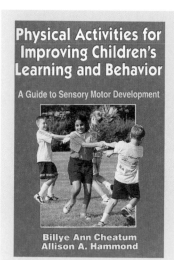

Physical Activities for Improving Children's Learning and Behaviour
by Billye Ann Cheatum + Allison A. Hammond, Human Kinetics, ISBN 0-88011–874-1

Full of ideas of activities, this book explains the underlying sensory-motor difficulties of many children and 'provides teachers and parents with a comprehensive approach to working with children who have learning or behaviour problems, – special attention is given to promoting sensory motor development.' Jean L. Pyfer, PhD, Texas Woman's University

Jumping and Bouncing

Children often love bouncing on the bed or settee. Parents often don't like it. But jumping stimulates all of a child's body with the high impact on their joints providing a whole body experience. Some children really need this kind of activity, which means that you may not be successful in stopping them from jumping.

A small TRAMPOLINE is a great piece of play-equipment (available from Argos). It allows the child to jump and the parent to be positive and say 'Yes, jump HERE!' The child can burn off energy, you can make it into an interactive rhythm-game, – or use it for your own home-fitness-training. If you buy a small round trampoline with short legs, it can also be put away easily under the bed or behind the settee, when enough is enough.

Children who do a lot of jumping need plenty of opportunity to do rhythmic, sensory and structured activities

Jumping Games

→ *Trampoline*
→ *Jumping off low walls when outdoors*
→ *Ball pool*
→ *On a therapy ball (with adult help)*
→ *Falling into a beanbag chair*
→ *Jump onto different carpet-squares/ into hoola hoops/ paving stones/ hankies spread out on carpet*
→ *Hopscotch*
→ *Jumping Jacks*
→ *Skipping rope: run under or jump over rope placed on/held a little above the ground, wiggly snake, run/jump through rope being turned by 2 adults*
→ *Sack race*
→ *Bounce on a Hippity Hop ball (big ball with handles)*
→ *Jumping rope: jump over rope held low, run through*

Ball pools allow a child to get his fill of jumping as well as having fun together.

Trampoline games

→ *Up and down counting to 3/5/10, then stop*
  • *turning while jumping*
  • *arms out to side at each jump*
  • *arms out in front*
  • *clap above head – arms down*
→ *Star jumps*
→ *Soldiers*
→ *Scissor jumps: scissoring one foot forward, with hands on hips*
  • *with arms up and down*
→ *Open – close legs with hands on hips*
  • *with arms out and in*
  • *with arms up and down*
→ *Running in place – fast, slow, first fast – then slow*
→ *From one foot to the other*
→ *Lift knees up high*

A small trampoline can be used by everyone in the family for exercises as well as for sensory and interactive play.

Pressure and Squeezing

Deep pressure to the body has a calming and grounding effect on many children that brings their whole sensory system into balance. Such slow, firm and predictable physical contact provides a containing sense of their body boundaries. Because it is such an organising experience, deep pressure activities are often useful to start off a play session.

Gym ball can be used in many ways, including sitting on while squeezed into a corner.

Pressure and Squeezing Activities

→ 'Bear hugs': wrap your arms around the child's body and arms to hug child tightly to your chest
→ Give child firm calming pressure on the shoulders
→ Head squeeze: place your hands on the sides of child's head above the ears and gently apply firm pressure
→ Wrap child tightly into towel after bath
→ Play dough: squashing, cutting, making pretend food, sausage, snakes, other animals
→ Plasticine: harder than play dough, which provides more sensory input, and more creative/symbolic opportunities
→ Quiet squeeze toys (avoid those with annoying squeaky noises)
→ Chew on refrigerator tubing: cut the tubing into 2- to 3-inch strips, or buy a 'chewy'
→ Squash bubble wrap
→ Gym ball games, e.g. have child hold therapy ball with arms and legs while lying on his/her back. Try to take the ball away and tell the child to hold on to the ball as hard as he can.

Some children love the sensation of being hugged tightly or being 'squeezed', which gives them feel 'held together'

Therapy ball

→ Lying over it on belly – going forwards and backwards
  • touch child's head and then feet on the floor
  • child reaching out with his hands to touch the ground side to side
  • hold child's feet, child stretches arms out to the side to become a bird/plane
  • pound short rhythm on side of ball for child to feel vibrations
  • bounce child with your hand on his back
  • get him to pick up balls/beanbags to toss into a bucket further away
→ 'Lying over it on back – as above
→ 'Lean against ball like a plank with feet on floor, to look at a book/ toss a ball
→ 'Sitting on ball:
  • bounce child up and down, side to side, counting to 10
  • bounce/roll child in rhythm to a rhyme/song
→ 'Adult sitting on it with child on lap
→ 'Child lying on his back on the floor:
  • roll ball over child like a 'sandwich'
  • passing ball with his hands from behind head to his feet onto floor and back
→ 'Child sitting on the floor – roll ball between 2-4 players
→ 'Walk across the room rolling the ball with one/alternate hands

Gym balls are more fun for a young child, when used together with an adult, thus supporting interactive movement play

Lots of ideas from 'Therapy Ball Activities Card Deck', Super Duper Publications, FD 115

Deep Pressure Activities
→ 'Sausage': roll child up in a mat, rug or heavy blanket
→ 'Sandwich': between cushions, mattress, or roll therapy ball over child lying on the floor
→ 'Hamburger': mat on the floor for 'bottom piece of bun', child lies on top as 'burger', heavy mat/cushion on top for 'top piece of bun', – other children can be added to lie on top as 'lettuce, onions, tomato, …' to increase sense of pressure. Rule: everyone must lie still like the burger/lettuce … (bouncing or jumping is not allowed)
→ 'Pizza' – child lies on his front: roll big ball over him to roll out pizza dough, pat into place, spread with tomato, sprinkle with cheese,
→ 'Wall push-ups': the idea of 'the room feels small this morning, can everyone help me push the walls out'

A stiff carpet can easily be rolled up to become a tunnel to crawl through.

Pushing, Pulling and Moving Things
The experience of muscle-tension that comes with making an effort has an organising effect, that can improve attention, arousal levels, body awareness and muscle tone, especially for children with low muscle-tone or hyper-activity issues.

Effortful and 'Heavy Weight' activities
→ Carrying: a heavy box , big nappy bag/ bag of potatoes/ other grocery bags, stacking/lifting/moving chairs/ books/boxes, bucket of water, – empty bin and waste-paper baskets
→ Moving: shopping trolley in supermarket, laundry basket, vacuum cleaner, heavy suitcase, sweeping, mopping, raking leaves, using wheel-barrow, tug-of-war, scooter-board, like-a-bike, scooter, lizard crawl
→ Sweeping, mopping, raking leaves, dustpan-and-brush
→ Scrubbing and cleaning sink, bath, dirty saucepans, doing washing-up using sponge, brush, …
→ 'Driving Miss Daisie': standing behind child 'drive' him with hands on his shoulder, – red, green, slow, fast
→ Wheelbarrow: pick up child's legs for them to walk on their hands with straight arms
→ Dump-truck: child holds another child around their waist, both facing the same way, and drags them to the 'dump'
→ Playing with something heavy, e.g. play 'catch' with heavy cushion, bag of oranges/ potatoes; – build tower with food tins
→ Digging and shoveling: sand, earth, gravel, stones, snow
→ Wrestling, e.g. 'Hat-stealing wrestling' (hold each other's right hands and try to steal the other person's hat)

Sweeping is a complex skill that involves the use of a tool, most children love using a big broom.

Moving heavy boxes involves motivation, making an effort and having a sense of direction.

→ Carry beanbags on shoulders/ head and walk across the room
→ Wear heavy backpack/ bum-bag to school, to carry shopping (books, drinks, vegetables, ...)
→ Wearing: weighted vest/blanket/belt, ankle/wrist weights

Shopping Game

→ Collect 'shopping': tins of food/potatoes/ books, box of cereal, washing powder, crate of juice cartons
→ You also need: a big sturdy box/container as 'shopping trolley' (big cardboard box works well)
→ Make cards with picture/word of each 'shopping' item
→ Place/hide 'shopping' around the room: on the chair, under the table, behind the door, on top of cupboard
→ Ask child to push 'trolley' to you to pick up one card from you, and then to collect shopping item, then return
→ When trolley is full, take shopping ... to another room/ back to the kitchen

If you have a wall to paint, why not cover the floor with plastic sheeting and get your child to do it?

Pushing and Pulling Activities

→ 'Row, row, row your boat' both sitting on the floor, pushing and pulling each other with the song
→ Blanket ride: pull child sitting on a blanket, let child pull sibling
→ Pushing-pulling: laundry basket, vacuum cleaner, heavy boxes,
→ Tug-of-war
→ Scooter-board
→ Balance bike, scooter
→ Lizard crawl (see Animal Walks)
→ Scooter board
→ Play 'cars' under the table: child pushes car with one hand while creeping and weight bearing on the other hand

Scooter board

→ Scooter board to and from a designated location (sit or lie on stomach and propel with arms)
→ Push sibling around on a wheeled chair or scooter board.
→ Pull someone while they sit on a scooter board holding onto a hula hoop.
→ Child can pull himself/herself up a ramp while on a scooter board.
→ Propel scooter board across carpeted floor.

Lots of ideas from 'Scooter Board Activities Card Deck', Super Duper Publications, FD 112

Balance, Swinging and Spinning Activities

Located in the inner ear, the balance sense or vestibular system is the most important sensory system as it coordinates all the others. It tells us where our body is in space, so we can maintain the posture that is necessary to move purposefully in order to do something. While movements like spinning, jumping and stop-start activities are arousing, i.e. they wake up a child, slow swinging or rocking can be calming and regulating for a child.

→ Balancing on a small wall in the park, on a plank, bench, beam, rope, line
→ Swinging in a blanket: 2 adults holding both sides of a blanket to swing child
→ Swings in the park: swing, twist-and-spin
→ Gym ball
→ Balance bike
→ Wobble board
→ Standing on one leg 'Tree position': how long?
→ Hopping on one leg, e.g. chalk-square hopping games
→ Spinning in a Snow Saucer
→ Balancing tube: roll a marble into middle of kitchen-roll tube to keep it there

Spinning a child on a circular 'snowsaucer' from: Cheatum & Hammond, Physical Activities for Improving Children's Learning and behaviour, page 66

Children love swinging in a blanket. Increase the communicative demands you make by waiting for the child to hand you the corners of the blanket, or to indicate for you to get up, either by gesture or words.

Seeing and Visuo-Spatial Activities

Visual problems are among the 'hidden disabilities' that often go undetected. In fact more than a quarter of children with learning or behavioural problems have underlying visual processing difficulties, even though they have been measured as having perfect 20/20 vision. But their brains cannot make sense of what their eyes are telling them, e.g. to sort out the difference between foreground and background, forms, sizes, distance, speed, position in space. If you want to find out more, you'll find a very helpful chapter in the book by Cheatum and Hammond (see beginning of this chapter).

The EYES do the LOOKING, but it is the BRAIN that does the SEEING.

Activities with Balloons
→ *bat with a cake tin (makes a satisfying clanging noise), with rolled up newspaper, with rolling pin*
→ *bat with hands, 10x without it touching the ground*
→ *bat balloon from person to person*
→ *make balloon squeak and whine after its been blown up by stretching the nozzle at the end*
→ *keep balloon in the air for as long as possible*
→ *pad balloon back and forth between players for as long as possible*
→ *let balloon whiz away*

It's magic! How can such a small thing become blown up so big so quickly?

Visual-Spatial Activities

→ Balloon games: blowing, batting, tracking, holding, catching, squeezing

→ 'Scarf toss': toss and catch 1 (or 2) silk scarves, – do it sitting, standing, jumping for it; toss to each other

→ 'Stack the cans': build tower or pyramid with food tins (they are heavy and good for hand-eye coordination)

→ Water and 'messy' play: in a shallow tray on the table (also corn-flour, sand, lentils, rice), in the bath using empty shampoo bottles, helping with washing up, ...

→ Blowing games: blow cardboard tubes across table, feathers to keep them in the air, bubbles

→ Skittles: use empty plastic bottles/ tins of food and a tennis ball to roll/toss to knock them over

→ Throwing and catching: bean-bag, teddy, cushion, big/small ball; throw-and-score: throw into target, bucket, ...

→ Jump rope: walk on it without falling off, child tries to jump onto 'wiggly snake', jump over rope held low, turn for child to run under

→ Wiggling snake: move rope like a snake for child to jump

→ 'Hide and seek': child hides and you find him; sibling hides and you search for them together; or you hide

→ 'Fishing games': fish leaves out of a pond or corks floating in bath/bucket with a tea-strainer; metal objects with a magnet at the end of a string 'fish' (or pictures with paper-clips attached)

→ Torch games (in a dark room/outdoors at night, – needs 2 torches): play 'catch me!' with each other's lights; 'follow me – follow you': draw a figure with child following your light-lines; 'Can you find the window?' with your torch: trace around window, door, picture, chair, table, ...; 'Jump into my circle': shine circle onto floor for child to jump in

→ 'Concept-hunt': walk around house together and find everything red/yellow, how many chairs/chair-legs?

→ Treasure Hunt: hide objects for child to find

→ Spatial and quantity concepts, e.g. here, there, gone, lots, little, more, ...
   1. Finding mum, shoes, chairs, socks ... in different parts of the house
   2. Negotiating 1 vs. 3 cars, biscuits, raisins, bits of apple, carrot, sweets, ...
   3. Showing with hands the difference between 'a little' and 'a lot'

→ Bingo and Picture Lotto games

→ 'Lazy eight': standing child traces a 'lazy 8' (= an 8 lying on its side) with a chalk or crayon

→ Building complex structures from visual cues: blocks, lego, copy a model: green-red ... blue-red-orange ...

→ Visualisation exercises: close your eyes and think of/imagine ...

'Stack the cans': use tins of food from your kitchen cupboards to play and build towers with. They are heavier than most toys, so your child will have a different experience

A shallow tray for sensory activities with sand or water, that siblings can join in with. Provide small scoops and some small containers for transferring stuff from here to there

Cornflour with a little bit of water. Have a wet cloth ready for wiping hands

Treasure hunt games

The aim is systematic searching:

→ hide 3 favorite objects in the room/ in the whole flat/ outdoors with child looking

→ hide things high up to encourage child to look up and around

→ hide things without child watching you

→ increase the number of objects for him to find

→ find 4 red/blue/green ... things, – all the red/blue/green things he can find

→ find 5 books/pens ... big/small/heavy things ...

→ describe in words: 'Your train is upstairs ... in the small green box under dad's bed.' (for children with speech comprehension: don't do this with children who are not yet on this level, because it will be confusing and frustrating)

→ find something to brush your hair with ... you need to go out (shoes, coat) ...

→ find something that makes sound ... that belongs to daddy ... is made from wood/ glass/ cloth ...

Everyday 'treasure-hunt': Getting things out of the fridge involves listing, reaching, looking, lifting and motor-planning.

Sensory Activities involving Touch

Some children love to have parts of their body massaged, stroked or brushed. Others don't like to be touched, but for them the repeated experience of massage of brushing might help with their sensory difficulties or 'tactile defensiveness'.

Massage and brushing can also help with body awareness, learning the parts of the body and building trusting relationships. In fact the skin is our largest sensory organ as well as responsible for 25% of detoxification every day, and regular brushing or massaging is calming to our nervous system and good for all of us.

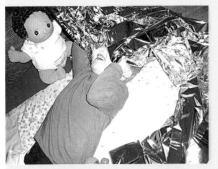

A rescue blanket is also great for sensory and interactive play: it is shiny, it crinkles, it lends itself to peekaboo and other hiding games.

Tactile and body-awareness activities

→ Name parts of the body while you massage/brush them; ask child 'where?' and wait for child to tell you by lifting up their leg/arm, later in words) which part of the body he wants brushed/massaged

→ Body-part tag: 'I'm going to touch … your …(build up expectant waiting) … hand, knee, foot, chin …! Or change roles: 'Don't touch my … arm, foot …!'

→ Tactile and sensory activities, e.g. put water, rice, lentils, cornflour … in a tray to feel; helping with washing up and cleaning the sink/bath/floor …

→ 'Treasure Hunt in a Jar': fill a big jar (could be transparent, but doesn't have to be) with lentils/rice/sand and hide 1-5 small objects in it (small car, buttons, marble, …) for child to find with his hand

→ Drawing in sand with finger/stick or on paving stones using water (best done in summer)

Drawing with water on paving stones using leaves or a brush

Massage and Brushing Box

→ *collect 5-8 different brushes (soft, harder), massage gloves, loofah, …*

→ *in a suitable box or container*

→ *use slow and firm reassuring stroking touch (note: fast and light tough can be very irritating!)*

→ *massage oils and aroma-therapy oils (lavender, …)*

Sequence of massaging or brushing:

1. *back of fore arms and hands*
2. *feet, especially the sole of the foot*
3. *front of legs up to the knee, back of legs up to the knee*

Oral Motor Activities

Some children have difficulties to use the muscles around their mouths effectively or to coordinate movement of their jaw, lips, tongue, breath and voice. This can affect a child's eating experience as well as their learning to speak.

→ Blowing, licking, chewing, sucking

→ Blowing: kitchen roll/ feather/ small paper-ball/ play dough ball/ pencil across the table, to each other

→ Licking: sticking tongue out in front of mirror, to lick jam from nose/chin/ out of egg-cup

→ Chewing, especially crunchy things, e.g. apple, cucumber, meat, raw carrot

→ Sucking from different kinds of straws: thick, curly-whirly, thin straws; thick milk-shake through a thick straw; suck up small pieces of paper with the straw and drop into a container

→ 'Blow table tennis': blow small ball/cotton wool/ tissue

'Blow-table tennis': Blowing a piece of paper, cotton wool or toilet roll across a table

Body Gymnastics and Movement Games

Rough-and-tumble and other gross-motor play is familiar to most parents, especially dads who are often great players of this kind of play that combines many of the underlying sensory systems.

→ Piggy back ride, 'horsy game'
→ Walking and running activities: rhythms, stop-start, slow-fast, up/down slopes, with a metronome
→ Airplane: child flying on dad's legs, with dad lying on his back (see example in baby section)
→ 'Angels in the snow': child lies on his back and moves his arms and legs as if making 'angels in the snow'; ask child only to move his left/right side, his arms/legs, his left arm and right leg, his right arm and left leg
→ Crawling through tunnel, rolled up carpet, lined up chairs
→ 'Tunnel of legs': child crawls through legs of people standing up
→ Climbing
→ 'Sword-fighting': use cardboard rolls or pipe-covering made from foam for practice pretend fight, managing strong feelings of anger, aggression, fear
→ Animal walks

Body-gymnastics involve lots of interaction and communication.

Rough and tumble games are familiar to most parents. Let the child add his ideas. The more, the better.

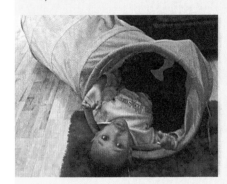

A fold-up tunnel for crawling, going in and out, and playing with there and gone, with loss and re-union.

Horse and rider games

Help the child, step by step, to understand the situation and to empathise with the horse. The overall story includes an endless variety of imaginary elements about the horse's feelings:

→ Start with simple rhythms of movement: let the child climb up, then wait for him to cue you to go. … Let him slide off, and start again …

→ Throw your rider off onto settee … then wait for him to come to you, climb up and cue you to go …

Later, when the child is beginning to understand language:

→ The horse is TIRED, and breaks down: what can the child do to help/get the horse back up? Does stroking it help? Where, – behind the ears, the head …? Or patting its back?

→ The horse is FED-UP and throws its rider off onto the settee: what now? Is the horse SAD? What will make the horse feel better? Or ANGRY? What is he cross about? Or AFRAID? What of?

→ The horse is THIRSTY and needs IMAGINARY water. Where can the child find some? What can he give as a container? Is the container too small (an upside lego) or too big (the horse can't reach) …?

→ The horse is HUNGRY. What can the child give the horse to eat? Does the horse like it (e.g. a puzzle piece, a book, …)? Yes? No? Then what?

→ The horse is EXCITED, … and throws the rider off and jumps away. What now?

→ The horse is AT HOME in its stable. How can the child entice it to come out? Will some grass tempt it? Or a carrot? Does the horse like carrots? What if it is offered an apple AND a carrot? (stay with pretend, if possible, rather than getting real food!)

When the autistic child drapes himself' onto the adult's back to avoid face-to-face interaction, we can often transform this into a 'horsey-game'

At first the 'horse' may move forward before throwing the child off, so she has to climb on again and giddy up the horse

As the child moves up the developmental ladder, the game becomes more symbolic: the horse is thirsty or tired, and has opinions as to what is on offer

Animal Walks

Animal walks practice lots of movements and can help to overcome retained reflexes as well as being fun.

→ Bear – keep arms and legs straight
  - put your hands and feet flat on the floor, rounding your back
  - walk slowly, rolling from side to side.
  - Move in this order: right arm
  - right foot
  - left arm
  - left foot

→ Crocodile – crocodiles are flat on the ground at all times. When they move forward, they wobble side to side.
  - child lying facedown on the ground with arms bent
  - move forward by extending one arm and bend the same-side leg forward, then other side
  - roll onto your back and try to move in the same way (real crocodiles would use their tails to flip the right way up again, like a tortoise would use its neck)

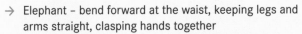

→ Elephant – bend forward at the waist, keeping legs and arms straight, clasping hands together
  - arms are now a trunk and cannot become unclasped unless in the event of serious elephant illness.
  - walk slowly, waving your trunk from side to side
  - swing your trunk low to touch your ankles.
  - pick some grass with your trunk and hold it up to your mouth.
  - lift your trunk high into the air to spray water everywhere
  - hold elephant trumpeting competitions
  - draw lying 8 with his 'trunk' (his arms)

→ Frog – squat down with your feet apart
  - put your hands on the floor in front of you and transfer your weight to them.
  - arms are straight on the ground between your knees and your weight is on them
  - extend the legs in a quick motion to propel body
  - stick out tongue

→ Crab - upside down on all fours, i.e. with tummy up
  - Walk forwards, backwards, sideways
  - Keeping one hand on the same spot walk in a circle around it
  - Move a ball through the room with dominant foot
  - Kick ball into a goal

→ Giraffe – extend arms straight up next to your ears and hook your thumbs together to form a giraffe head.
  - keeping legs straight, walk around on your tiptoes for maximum height.
  - slowly bend forward and 'drink' with the giraffe head.
  - legs must stay straight and the arms are always alongside the ears.

→ Inch worm – moves by bending its entire body in half, drawing up the back then stretching out the front.
  - get down on all fours, putting your weight evenly on your hands and feet.
  - with back arched and your arms and legs straight, walk your hands forward until your back is straight
  - walk your feet forward until they are as close as they can get to your hands without bending your knees

→ Camel – cross your arms behind your back and hold opposite elbows
  - bend forwards at the waist, keeping your head up and your eyes straight ahead
  - walk slowly, lifting your heels up behind following each step.
  - keep some distance so you don't get kicked
  - make a (suitably spaced) camel train

→ Kangaroo – keep both legs together at all times.
  - place a beanbag/ cushion between your knees and don't drop it.
  - hold up your arms close to your chest with elbows bent and palms facing forwards
  - jump around the place, or follow a specific paths, while holding that position.

→ Rabbit – squat down, move your arms forward together and put them on the floor in front of you.
  - shift weight onto your hands.
  - jump feet forward until they are between your hands, keeping hands on the ground
  - rabbit hop through a hoop

→ Puppy – get down on all fours and distribute your weight evenly, bending legs and elbows
  - lift your head so eyes are forward and scamper around like a playful puppy

→ Dog – get down on all fours and distribute your weight evenly, bending legs and elbows
  - synchronize opposite arm and leg, i.e. left arm and right leg, and vice versa
  - stretch arms and legs for 'upside down dog' (Yoga), – get dog to lift one leg in male dog fashion

→ Cat – on all fours, the cat arches her back with head and eyes down,
  - then lifts head up and hollows the back (Yoga)

→ Seal – lie down flat on a mat with your elbows bent, your legs straight
  - hands on the floor, palms down, at about your shoulder level
  - put your weight on your arms so they are supporting your entire body
  - keeping your legs straight, use your arms to 'walk' and drag your toes along behind you.

→ Mule Kick – bend down from the waist and place your hands on the mat, palms down.
  - shift your weight to your palms, keep your feet together and kick them out behind you.

→ Chicken/ Cockerel – in a standing position reach behind you and grab your left foot with your right hand.
  - hop around for a bit – forwards and backward.
  - swap hand/foot so that you are holding your right foot in your left hand and standing on your left foot.

Your Home as your Playground

Sometimes NOT having toys can be a good thing and make play more social, engaging and imaginative. Even if you live in a small flat, there are many ways to use your environment for interactive play to support your child's communication and interactive play.

Doors, windows and curtains

DOORS can be used to play 'Open – shut! Open – shut!' or peekaboo or 'Knock knock, who's there?' or 'Can I come in? – No, you can't ... well ok then.' WINDOWS can become a lift with the curtains as 'doors' and are of course great to sit together looking out and talking about what you can see together.

→ **Doors:** open-shut, there-gone, 'knock-knock who's there?'
→ **Windows:** 'what can you see?', naming what you can see, e.g. cars, birds, people, planes, helicopter, moon
→ **Curtains:** peekaboo, open-shut, there-gone: to play 'house' or 'lift'

Tables, sofas, cushions and other furniture

SOFAS can become dark caves, if your child loves 'deep pressure' and you let him climb inbetween the seat-cushions, or you can use the cushions to build a tower, to play 'catch' or for a pillow-fight. Some leathery sofas allow you to make a small slide with the seat cushions. TABLES and CHAIRS are wonderful for playing. Not only can we use them to sit at to eat, draw, write and play. But a table can also become a house to sit inside (perhaps with a sheet over it) or a den, a car, a bus, ... A small table can be part of a simple OBSTACLE COURSE to help children learn about many things including sequences, spatial concepts (on, off, under, over, through, around, ...) and to burn off energy, especially when stuck indoors on rainy days.

→ **Sofa:** as a slide, squeeze games between cushions,
→ **Sofa cushions:** build a tower, 'catch', 'pillow fight', 'musical cushions'
→ **Table:** to hide under, to crawl through like tunnel, – with blanket/sheet over it to make a 'house'
→ **Coffee table:** upside down it can become a car, bus, boat to sit inside
→ **Chairs:** 2 chairs can become a 'house' with a blanket over them
→ **Swivel chair:** for spinning games, e.g. 'ready steady ...go!', 'round and round and ... STOP!'

Standing on the groundfloor window sill, he says 'Lift going up. Seventh floor. Doors opening'. On a post-it note dad has written 1-9 for each floor

Stuck at home in a tiny flat, this boy invented his own sofa-slide using the seat cushion

This coffee-table has become a car. But the 'driver' is unhappy about his brother joining him for the drive

Obstacle course

The sequence of this improvised obstacle course:
→ Walk along the balancing board
→ Climb up on the stool
→ Clap your hands 3x
→ Jump off
→ Crawl through the big box
→ Step through the hoop, – careful not to make it fall!
→ Bounce 3x on the cushion
→ Step off and turn around
→ Climb onto the chair
→ Jump off
→ And sit down by finishing line.
→ Wait for your brother/sister to have a turn.
→ And again …

Obstacle course from: Barbara Sher, Early Intervention Games: Fun, Joyful Ways to Develop Social and Motor Skills in Children with Autism Spectrum or Sensory Processing Disorders, 2009, Josse, ISBN 9780470391266

Blankets, rugs and carpets

BLANKETS can be used to swing or drag the child, to hide under, for peekaboo games or to become a 'house'. CARPETS can become a tunnel to crawl through. A firm RUG tends to be better than a blanket to roll up a child who likes deep pressure into a 'sausage'

→ 'Blanket car': drag child in a blanket across the floor, – 'go go go go … STOP!', 'Which way?'
→ Sausage game: roll child in blanket, rug, mat
→ Swinging in a blanket

Blanket-house made with 2 chairs to go in and out, to take things in and to hide inside.

Swinging games

Many children love SWINGING-games and you can use this to help your child to build up his communicative 'muscles'. Don't just give him a free ride! MAKE HIM WORK. Once you have swung him a few times, WAIT for him to give you the end of the blanket, to look at you or make a sound telling you what to do at every moment. Watch for his gestures and subtle communicative cues telling you to go 'UP' or what to sing.

Sausage game

A favourite of many young children, the SAUSAGE-GAME involves rolling the child up in a rug or blanket. Some children like the dark, others must have their head out so they don't feel trapped inside. See if you can wait for him to make a sound to tell you to unroll him again! Sometimes children like to feel pressure on their body when you sit on them gently.

Blanket-car to pull the child through the room . Ask him to point and tell you 'Which way?'

Shoes and slippers

SHOES can become wonderful play-things! Collect all the shoes in your house to put into a box as a POSTING activity: 'IN and IN and IN … and all OUT again! And again: IN and IN …' I have also done this activity using potatoes or onions or anything else that could be 'put in'.

Activities using shoes and slippers

→ **Posting and 'in-out' game**: Put everybody's shoes in a box as a basic activity of 'in and out'; throw them in from some distance

So many shoes and slippers! Who is going to pair and match them? Or line them up? Or sort them by size? Or colour?

→ **Matching and sorting**: match into pairs, sort by size, colour or owner, left and right, laces/Velcro, indoor/outdoor, trainers/sandals/boots …

→ **Place** neatly into shoe rack.

→ **'Shoe-jumping'**: child to jump over 1 shoe, then 2 shoes, then pile of shoes

→ **Symbolic and pretend play:** shoes can become cars and busses, – clothes pegs can become passengers, or connect several slippers to make a 'slipper-train'

Water play

Children love water. After all, this where we all came from before we were born! Water is a most fascinating play thing as it is always changing, inviting endless exploration, learning and play.

Water play can entertain children for a long time. Use a cat-litter tray, small scoops and containers, and some small stones for scooping

→ **Water tray:** Put some water in a shallow tray (with a towel underneath for spillages) with small containers for simple pouring, -with bubbles, sand, pebbles, …

→ **Water taps:** many children love to play with the taps to make the water run and stop 'open – closed', feeling it on their hands, watching it make patterns in the sink, disappear down the plug hole, filling small containers, …

→ **Bath play:** allow your child to sit in the bath for 30-45 minutes, – give him containers, empty shampoo bottles, strainers, which are better play value, because you can do more with them, than with ducks and boats (all they do is float)

→ **Doing the washing up:** combine your child's love for water with some of the daily chores. Cleaning a 'dirty' saucepan with brush or sponge is interesting, – seeing the food remnants come off, float in the water, go down or get stuck in the plug hole …

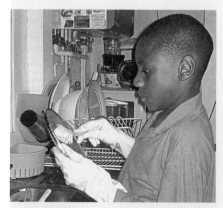

This boy can not speak. But he loves doing the washing up

→ **'Fishing games':** using a tool/strainer to 'fish' out objects floating in water

→ **Go swimming** together regularly: float with armbands or 'noodles', jump in, catch him, chase him, blow bubbles, …

→ **Puddles:** put waterproof boots on first, – then jump in, splash and make patterns, drag a branch or stick through the water, throw pebbles or twigs in, …
→ **Draw with water outdoors** on hot stones or on the pavement in the summer, using paint-brush/stick
→ **Water the plants** in the garden with a watering can or bucket

Fishing game
→ *Get a bucket/washing up bowl with water*
→ *and a bowl with ice cubes/ plastic ice cubes/ ping-pong balls (draw faces on them)/ corks/ polystyrene packing chips*
→ *empty balls/corks into water*
→ *ask your child to fish out balls with*
→ *a small strainer/ fishing net/ tongues and*
→ *place into empty bowl*

Games using Play-Materials
There are so many things in your house that cost no money, but that have a high 'play-value' for any child, often more so then many toys. Use them and don't let these fantastic opportunities go to waste!

Exploration, problem solving and fostering new ideas
Bringing up children in small flats means, that there MUST be sufficient 'Loose Parts' around for them to explore, play and occupy themselves with in order to develop their own thinking, imagination, creativity and language. This means that for a city-child's healthy mental development, the flat/house must NOT be immaculately tidy all day long with nothing lying around, otherwise the child cannot explore the world around him, which is crucial for every child's learning, and his mind is at risk of play-deprivation and mental starvation.

Loose Parts refers to anything that can be moved around, carried, rolled, lifted, piled on top of one another, or combined to create interesting and novel structures and experiences. Loose parts include wood, containers, shapes, toys, animals, plants, and so on. Loose parts allow children to take an object that has a loosely defined purpose and use it to be anything that they want for their playing. Thus a cardboard box can be a den or a car or an airplane, a bed or a tortoise shell. Loose parts do exactly the opposite of battery-powered toys that require the child only to push a button to send the toy into an ecstasy of beeping and flashing and tinny music.

Examples of 3 containers of 'Loose Parts' for indoor and outdoor play.

Such toys do the playing while the child is reduced to the passive role of an audience. Play itself, with these toys, is turned into a space of exclusion for children. They're kept outside the play circle, which is dominated by the moving toy. Loose parts liberate the imagination and creativity of the playing children and allow them to master the world around them in ever-changing ways and communicate more effectively through their playing.'

> Penny Wilson, The Play Work Primer, 2009, www.allianceforchildhood.org

Without cardboard tubes and pennies this boy would not have been able to invent this posting activity

During the day, there must be things around for the child to explore, combine and occupy himself with. They must be easily accessible, i.e. he must be able to reach and get them without having to ask an adult for help or permission. These can be toys, – but more important are 'non-toys' and creative materials that only become something with the child's exploration and imagination, e.g.

→ **Empty containers** of all sorts of shapes and sizes, e.g. egg boxes, yoghurt-pots, cartons, boxes, paper bags, food containers with lids, ...

→ **Natural materials**, e.g. conkers, pine cones, smooth pebbles/stones, autumn leaves, ...

→ **Space and time** to play without disturbance and interruption

→ **Enough paper and card board**

→ **Pencils/pens**

→ **Everyday objects**, e.g. blanket, scarf, sofa cushions, shoes, slippers, clothes pegs

→ **String, sellotape** and other materials to link/combine objects

→ **Scissors** will need to be kept safe and only used under an adult's supervision

Creative play using curtain rings, wooden clothes pegs, containers and a pair of kitchen tongs

Each of these must have a 'home', i.e. a drawer, a box or a space on a shelf 'where they live' and where they get tidied up to, again and again. It is best, if each child has their own private 'storage-space', that is easily accessible to the child, so they can find something to explore and do when they get bored, or when they have an idea.

Sorting activities are crucial for mental and language development. They can only happen, if there are enough small things and containers around. Egg boxes and recycled packaging materials will often do

Tidying up is a language activity

Every evening, and every now and again during the day, it will be time to TIDY UP and putting things 'where they go'. It helps if you don't see it as just a chore, or even as your child being 'bad' or 'messy'. Taking things out, re-organising them in his play and putting them back in is a child's 'job' and main learning task. Tidying up is a very important activity of picking up and letting go, sorting, categorizing for learning to think, understand and use language for talking.

Recycled materials

The empty packaging and containers we all produce every day are great play-materials, e.g. empty tissue boxes, toilet rolls, cereal packages, yoghurt pots, ice-cream containers, etc. Don't just throw them away, but keep them in a big box within easy reach so your child can use them for creative, explorative and imaginative play!

→ **Building towers**: with different size boxes and containers, food tins, tissue packets, toilet rolls, ...

→ **Box rides:** child sits in large cardboard box; push it around like a car; add paper-plate for steering wheel, a scarf as seat belt, draw a car-radio on the inside; rock 'the boat', tip it over; make into a 'bed' with a blanket and pillow ...

→ **Posting box:** cut a slit into an empty box to post cards/ coins; cut 4 slits and mark each with a colour for posting small squares of coloured card to match the 4 colours

→ **Box games:** making things out of recycled cardboard boxes, e.g. box becomes car/house/boat for teddy; cut out windows and door; have 2 boxes/homes so 2 teddies can visit each other

→ **Empty bottles:** shampoo and similar bottles to play with in the bath, make a shop

→ **Egg boxes** (see below)

Egg boxes

Egg boxes have become one of my favourite play-materials, because there is so much you can do with them! Not only can you use them to build towers and knock them over in different ways or put small things into their compartments. But they can also become a big mouth, a hat, a car, a train, a ship, a house (with a door cut into the top). Can you think of 10 more things you could do with your child using egg boxes?

A big cardboard box can become a house, a car, a shopping trolley, a boat ... or just a fun thing to sit in with the adult moving it along.

Making things from recycled cardboard boxes can involve the whole family in creative activity.

'Look at my egg box glasses.'

20 Things to do with Egg boxes

Egg boxes have recently become one of my favorite play-material, because there are just so many things you can do with them, from sensory-motor to problem-solving, symbolic, imaginary and pretend play. Here are some ideas for egg boxes (try to add 3 new ideas of your own and let me know!):

1. Collect about **10 egg boxes** (for 6 eggs)
2. Get the child to **open and close** them (that's simple problem- solving)
3. Open and close like a **mouth** and make it talk, e.g. 'Hello, I am an egg box mouth.' ...
4. Put small things (scrunched-up paper, stones, ...) into each little hole
5. Tear off top and wear like a **hat**.
6. **Stack** all the tops and all the bottoms.
7. **Poke holes** through each of the 6 egg-holders, – with a pencil, with your finger, ...
8. Build a **tower** and knock it down
9. Can you **blow it** down? Blow the top-box, – then blow the one   in the middle or the second ...
10. Make an egg box into **a car.** Put some onions, walnuts, lychees, socks, ... in as passengers. Where's the car going? Where's the petrol-station?
11. Have a **race** with different egg box-cars.
12. Make a **train.** How can you connect the carriages? Who's the driver? An onion will do ...
13. **Paint or draw** on the egg boxes: windows, doors, people looking out of the windows, ...
14. Stand an egg box on its front to make a **house**.
15. Connect several egg boxes to make a **dragon.**
16. Get some scissors and cut a door and windows into the top.   Can the child do it?
17. Who lives in your house? ... or the other egg box? Can they visit each other? 'Hello!'
18. Make **glasses** by tearing off 2 egg-cups and poking holes through and attach some string. Let your child try to find a way to attach the string.
19. Attach string to make it into a **camera** or binoculars, that you can wear round your neck
20. Fill an egg box with soil and **plant beans** into each hole.

Egg box monsters having a conversation and performing for the camera

'Look at my egg box train!', with clothes-pegs connecting the eggbox-carriages

Egg boxes and other recycled materials also allow a child to play creatively by themselves

Play materials, toys and games

Toys and play materials are a language that helps children to express themselves and to show us what they are thinking and interested in. But until the child with autism reaches the more symbolic developmental levels (FEDL 4-6), the interactive movement and people games described above will be most appropriate and helpful.

For more imaginative ideas and activities with toys and other play materials see 'Playing in the family', – after all the autistic child is also a child in a family, like any other child.

A set of sandwich boxes or 'food saver containers' with lids has fantastic play value: in – out, open – shut, sizes, matching, sorting, problem solving, making music (rattles, drum).

KEEP IT SIMPLE!
The more simple the play materials, the more imagination, creativity and language your child will develop.

WARNING!

Things to AVOID:
Don't have too many
→ pre-formed toys that leave little to the imagination
→ cars, trains or toys with wheels
→ electronic or press-the-button 'lazy toys'
→ branded toys from TV or video series

There is so much that can be done with wooden bricks (much more versatile than cheap plastic 'lego') as the require careful placing.

These little people are at school assembly with Shrek as their teacher.

Basic Set of Play-Materials

You don't actually need much in terms of toys and play materials in order to play meaningfully with your child. A few simple things are enough, – and usually even better than too many pre-formed toys that leave less to the imagination than a few recycled or cardboard boxes, which have infinite play-value. Here is a basic set of play materials:

1. **Large plastic tray** (about the size of an A4 paper): for holding and storing materials, for water or messy activities
2. **Set of 6-10 small trays/containers:** for sorting, pairing, matching, symbolic play
3. **Empty containers and bottles with tops:** matching, push-on and screw tops, on-off, in-out, problem-solving
4. **Set of food saver containers with lids** (at least 10 per pack of different sizes and shapes): sorting, playing shop
5. **Plasticine, play-dough, small tub of clay to roll**, squeeze, cut and make food, animals or people with
6. **Wooden bricks:** sorting by colour/shape, building towers, copying simple constructions

The best play materials are everyday objects

7. **Little people and animals:** families of little people or animals allow a child to play out his experience
8. **Doll and teddies:** to imitate child's own everyday experience of sleeping, eating, dressing, ...
9. **Toy tea set and cutlery:** for early symbolic play, also sorting, pairing, matching with real cups, spoons, forks
10. **Large clothes pegs:** different colours, clipping around a bowl, onto clothing, for fine motor skills, to connect boxes
11. **Enough paper and pens/pencils**
12. **Cotton reels, large beads and thick thread:** for threading, fine motor skills, hand-eye coordination
13. **Picture lotto game:** for matching pictures, listening, looking, learning to take turns
14. **'Like-a-Bike' or Balance Bike** (without pedals) for balance and coordination, using both sides of the body/brain (unlike scooters which are very one-sided), only to be used outdoors

Small trays for matching and sorting

Small containers for sorting

Cup tree

Multi-coloured stacker toy for sequencing

Pack of 10 washing-up sponges

Kitchen roll holder

Plastic bottle with lid for posting

Clothes pegs

Large beads and cord for threading

Small container of sand (with lid)

Hair bands

Dolly pegs

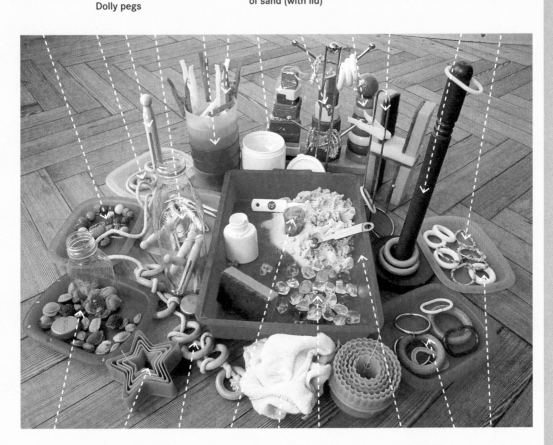

Pastry cutters for sequencing by size

Cloth for wiping hands and spillages

Small cat-litter tray for water/ sand play

Stones of apricots, peaches, plums for pincer-grip posting

Sand toys: small scoop, small containers

Piece of rope

Plastic aquarium crystals for putting in, posting, tranferring

Curtain rings, different sizes

Bibliography

ACQUERONE, S. (2004), *Infant Psychotherapy*. Karnac, London

AHMED, N. (2005), *Women in Between: A study of the Experiences of Bangladeshi Women Living in Tower Hamlets*. Nuffield Foundation/ Keele University

ALONIM, H. et al. (2002), *The Mifne Approach*. The Mifne Center – Early Intervention for the Treatment of Autism

ALVAREZ, A. (2001), *Live Company*. Routledge, London

ALVAREZ, A. et al. 1999), *Autism and Personality*. Routledge, London

BALBERNIE, R. (2001), *Circuits and Circumstances: the neurobiological consequences of early relationship experiences and how they shape later behaviour*. Journal of Child Psychotherapy, 27,3

BARRETT, M. (2004), *The Wisdom of Culture*. The Psychologist, 17,8

BION, W. (1962), *Learning from Experience*. London: Heinemann

BION, W. (1967/ 1984), *A theory of thinking*. In: Second Thoughts. London: Heinemann

BION, W. (1970/ 1984), *Attention and Interpretation*. London: Heinemann

BOWLBY, J. (1969), *Attachment and Loss*. London: Howgarth Press

BRAZELTON, B. (1992), *Touchpoints: Your child's emotional and behavioural development*. Penguin

BRAZELTON, B. &, GREENSPAN, S. (2000), *The Irreducible Needs of Children*. Cambridge/US: Perseus

BROUCEK, F. (1979), *Efficacy in infancy: a review of some experimental studies and their possible implications for clinical theory*. Int. J. Psych-An. 311.

BUNCE, KIM (2005), *Tough Love on Tap: Supernanny*. The Observer Magazine, 3.4.2005

CHEATUM, B. et al (2000), *Physical Activities for Improving Children's Learning and Behaviour. A Guide to Sensory Motor Development*. Human Kinetics

CHOWDHURY-ANWARULLAH (1995), *Families in Bangladesh*. Journal of comparative family studies, vol. 26,1, Canada

CRITTENDEN, P., & CLAUSSEN, A. (2000), *The organisation of attachment relationships*. Cambridge: University Press

DEKABAN, A.S., SADOWSKY, D. (1978), *Changes in brain weight during the span of human life*. Annual Neurology 4: 345-356

DELANEY, T. (2010), *101 Games and Activities for Children with Autism, Asperger's and Sensory Processing Disorder*. McGraw Hill Companies

DELION, P. (2000), *The application of Esther Bick's method to the observation of babies at risk of autism*. In: The International Journal of Infant Observation and its Applications, vol. 3, no.3

DOUGLAS, H. & & GINTY, M (2001), *The Solihull Approach: Evaluation of Changes in the Practice of Health Visitors*. In: Community Practitioner 74, 222-224

FLORANCE, C., (2005), *A Boy Beyond Reach*. Pocket Books.

FRAIBERG, S. (1997), *The Magic Years. Understanding and Handling the Problems of Early Childhood*. Simon @ Schuster

FONAGY, P. (2001), *Attachment theory and psychoanalysis*. New York: Other Press

FONAGY, P., GERGELY, G., JURIST, E., TARGET, M. (2002) , *Affect Regulation, Mentalization and the Development of the Self*. NY: Other Press

GERHARD, S. (2004), *Why love matters*. London: Routledge

GOLDSCHMIED, E. & JACKSON, S. (1994), *People Under Three*. London: Routledge

GOLDSCHMIED, E., *Babies at Work: The Treasure Basket*. Video: NCB

GOPNIK, A., KUHL, P., METZOFF, A. (2001*, How Babies Think*. Phoenix Books

GREENFIELD, S. (2009), *ID: The Quest for Identity in the 21st Century*. Scepter

GREENSPAN, S.I. & WIEDER, S. (1998), *The child with special needs: encouraging emotional and , intellectual growth*. Reading MA: Perseus

GREENSPAN et al. (1999), *Building healthy minds*. Perseus Books.

GREENSPAN, S.I. (2003), *The Clinical Interview of the Child*. Washington DC: American Psychiatric Publishing

GREENSPAN, S. &, SHANKER, S. (2004), *The First Idea*. Cambridge MA: Da Capo Press

GREENSPAN, S. et al. (2006), *Engaging Autism*. Da Capo Press Lifelong

HOBSON, P. (1993), *Autism and the development of mind*. Hove: Lawrence Erlbaum

HOBSON, P. (2004), *The Cradle of Thought*. Pan Books. London

HOLMES, J. 2001, *The search for the secure base*. Hove: Brunner-Routledge

JANERT, S. (1995), *Play in the first 6 months*. Nursery World, 16.2.1995

JANERT, S. (2000), *Reaching The Young Autistic Child*. London: Free Association Books

JANERT, S. (2004), *In the Family: Effective Parenting and Behaviour Management*. London: SureStart on the Ocean

JANERT, S., HAWKINS, M., COATES, S. (2006) *Autism in the Family*. Picturebook with flaps to open. MindBuilders

JANERT, S. (2007), *Psychoanalytisches Denken nach Hause bringen. Eltern als Partner mit ihrem autistischen Kind*. In: Frühe Beziehungserfahrungen. Psychosozial Verlag

KAPLAN, M. (2006), *Seeing through New Eyes*. Jessica Kingsley, London

KARR-MORSE, R. & WILEY, M. (1997), *Ghosts from the Nursery: Tracing the roots of violence*. NY: The Atlantic Monthly Press

KLEIN, M. (1985), *The Writings of Melanie Klein*. London: Howgarth Press

KRANOWITZ, CAROL (2005), *The Out-of-Synch Child*. Penguin NY

KRANOWITZ, CAROL (2004), *The Goodenoughs get in Sync*. Sensory Resources, Las Vegas

LECHEVALIER, B. et al. (2000), West's Syndrome and Infantile Autism: the Effect of a Psychotherapeutic Approach in Certain Cases. In: In: International Journal of Infant Observation, 3,3

LEIDERMANN, P., TULKIN, S., ROSENFELD, A. (1977), , *Culture and Infancy*. New York: , Academic Press

LEVINE, (1977), *Childrearing as cultural adaptation*. In: Leidermann, P., Tulkin, S., Rosenfeld, A.: Culture and Infancy

LORD, C. et al. (2001), *Educating Children with Autism*. National Research Council. National Academy Press. Washington DC

MAIN, M., KAPLAN, N. & CASSIDY (1985), *Security in infancy, childhood and adulthood: A move to the level of representation*. Monographs of the Society for Research in Child Development, 50, , 60-104.

MARSHALL 2004), *A community psychologist working in SureStart*. Newsletter of the Association for Infant Mental Health, 4,1

MELTZER, D. (1975), *Explorations in Autism*. Strath Tay: Clunie Press

MELTZER, D. (1986), *Studies in Extended Metapsychology*. Strath Tay: Clunie Press

MELTZER, D. (1988), *The Apprehension of Beauty*. Strath Tay: Clunie Press

MELTZER, D. (1994), *Sincerity and other works*. London: Karnac Books

MILLER,L., RUSTIN,M., RUSTIN,M., SHUTTLEWORTH, S. (1993), *Closely observed infants.* London: Duckworth & Co.

MOORE, J. (2008*), Playing, laughing and learning with children on the autistic spectrum.* Jessica Kingsley, London

NADESAN, M. (2005), *Constructing Autism. Unravelling the 'truth' and understanding the social.* Routledge.

NEGRI, R. (1994), *The Newborn in the Intensive Care Unit.* London: Karnac Books

NEWBERGER, E. (1980), *Parental Awareness Measure (PAM)*

PANKSEPP, J (1988), *Affective neuroscience: the foundations of human and animal emotions.* NY

PERRY, B. et al. (1995), Childhood Trauma, the Neurobiology of Adaptation, and 'Use-dependent' Development of the Brain: How 'States' Become 'Traits'. Infant Mental Health Journal. Vol. 16, 4

PERRY, B.D. (1997), *Incubated in Terror: Neurodevelopmental factors in the 'cycle of violence'.* In: Osofsky, J.D. (ed.) Children in a violent society. New York: Guilford Press

RAHMAN, Shahidun (2004), *Ibrahim.* Writers World, Oxford

RAMEY,C.T., & RAMEY,S.L. (1998). *Early intervention and early experience.* American Psychol., 53(2), 109-120

RINGER, M. (2002), *Group Action.* London: Jessica Kingsley

SCABBIOLO, F., *Personal communication*

SCHORE, A. (1994), *Affect Regulation And The Origin Of The Self: The Neurobiology of Emotional Development.* NJ: Lawrence Erlbaum Associates

SOLOMON, R.(2004), *A Journey of Hope. Play and Language for Autistic Youngsters: The P.L.A.Y. Project Workshop Level 1, DVD*

SOLOMON, R. et al. (2007), *Pilot Study of a Parent Training Program for Young Children with Autism: The P.L.A.Y. Project Home Consultation Program.* In: Autism: The International Journal of Research and Practice.

SOLOMON, W. et al. (2012), *Autism and Understanding. The Waldon Approach to Child Development.* Sage

STERN, D. (1977), *The first relationship: Infant and Mother.* Cambridge MA: Harvard

STERN, D. (1985), *The Interpersonal World Of The Infant.* New York: Basic Books

STERN, D. (1990), *Diary of a Baby: What your child sees, feels and experiences.* Harper Collins

STEWART, S., BOND, M., ABDULLAH, A., MA, S., (2000)), *Gender, Parenting And Adolescent Functioning in Bangladesh.* Merrill-Palmer Quarterly, 46, 3

STONE, M.K. (1995), *Don't Just Do Something, Sit There.* Religious and Moral Education Press

STROH, K. (2008), *Every Child Can Learn. Using Learning Tools and play to help children with developmental delay.* Sage

SUNDERLAND, M. (2007), *What every Parent Needs to Know.* Dorling Kindersley,

TREVARTHEN, C. (1974), *Conversations With A 2 Month Old.* New Scientist

TREVARTHAN,C. (1980), *The Foundations Of Intersubjectivity.* In: D.R.Olson (Ed.): The Social , Function Of Language And Thought. New York: Norton

TREVARTHEN,C. (1984), *Emotions In Infancy.* In: Scherer, K.& Ekman, P. (Eds.) Approaches to Emotion. Hillsdale, NJ: Erlbaum

TREVARTHAN, C.& HUBLEY, P.(1978), *Secondary Intersubjectivity: Confidence, Confiders And , Acts Of Meaning In The First Year.* In: A. Lock (Ed.): Action, Gesture and Symbol. NY: Academic Press and The Institute Of Psycho-Analysis.

TREVARTHEN , C. (1988), *Infants Trying To Talk: How A Child Invites Communication from the Human World*. In: Children's Creative Communication, Ed. R. Soederbergh, Lund University Press, Sweden

TREVARTHEN, C. (1984), *Emotions In Infancy.* In: Scherer, K.& Ekman, P. (Eds.) Approaches To Emotion. Hillsdale, NJ: Erlbaum

TUSTIN, F. (1986), *Autistic Barriers in Neurotic Patients.* London: Karnac

TUSTIN, F. (1990), *The Protective Shell in Children and Adults.* London: Karnac

URWIN, C. (2003), *Breaking Ground, Hitting Ground.* Journal of child psychoth. 29,3

WARD, A. (2001), *Do babies think?* – Presentation on 26.9.2001 at a CAMHS study day

WEBSTER-STRATTON, C. (1992), *The Incredible Years: A trouble-shooting guide for parents of children ages 3-8 years.* Toronto: Umbrella Press.

WINNICOTT, D. 1965), *The Maturational Processes and the Facilitating Environment.* London: Howgarth Press